Answer Keys

Unit 1 | Language

Practice 1

Target iBT TOEFL Questions

1. Ⓐ 2. Ⓑ 3. Ⓑ 4. Ⓑ

iBT TOEFL Vocabulary

1. respond
2. copy
3. complete
4. exaggerate
5. toddler

Wrap Up

Ⓐ

1. exaggerate
2. toddler
3. responded
4. copying
5. complete

Ⓑ

Paragraph 1: ①-④-⑤-②-③
Paragraph 2: exaggerate, louder, high pitched

Practice 2

Target iBT TOEFL Questions

1. Ⓒ 2. Ⓐ 3. Ⓑ 4. Ⓑ

iBT TOEFL Vocabulary

1. location   2. inborn   3. raise
4. definitely 5. limited 6. regularly

Wrap Up

Ⓐ

1. an inborn   2. location   3. raised
4. definitely 5. a limited 6. regularly

Ⓑ
1. (c)   2. (b)   3. (a), (d)

Test 1 The History of Writing

1. Ⓑ 2. Ⓒ 3. Ⓐ 4. Ⓒ 5. Ⓑ
6. Ⓑ 7. Ⓑ

Test 2 Artificial Language

1. Ⓒ 2. Ⓐ 3. Ⓑ 4. Ⓒ 5. Ⓓ
6. Ⓓ 7. Ⓐ 8. Ⓐ 9. Ⓑ

Reading Helper

A

1. NASA   2. Eskimos   3. Socrates

B

1. Nothing is as effective as face-to-face communication.
2. Some animals are as emotional as human beings.
3. Average stars are not as bright as the Sun.

Unit 2 | Agriculture

Practice 1

Target iBT TOEFL Questions

1. Ⓑ 2. Ⓐ

iBT TOEFL Vocabulary

1. artificial   2. apply
3. beneficial   4. conventional
5. controversy   6. exposure

Wrap Up

Ⓐ

1. artificial   2. beneficial
3. controversy 4. conventional
5. exposure   6. applied

B

Traditional, chemicals, natural, organic, 70, cost, exposure

Practice 2

Target iBT TOEFL Questions

1. Ⓒ   2. Ⓑ

iBT TOEFL Vocabulary

1. demand   2. overuse   3. manufacture
4. control   5. particular   6. resource

Wrap Up

A

1. demand   2. particular   3. manufactures
4. resources   5. controlled   6. overuse

B

rivers, nutrients, 75, glaciers, Causes, car, 2025

Test 1   Bird Flu

1. Ⓒ   2. Ⓑ   3. Ⓒ   4. Ⓓ   5. Ⓒ
6. Ⓐ   7. Ⓑ

Test 2   DDT

1. Ⓓ   2. Ⓐ   3. Ⓒ   4. Ⓒ   5. Ⓐ
6. Ⓐ   7. Ⓐ   8. Ⓑ

Reading Helper

A

1. High-fiber foods such as beans and vegetables take longer to digest.
2. The file includes the details of the plan such as purposes and strategies.
3. People are starting to look at alternative energy such as solar or wind power.

B

1. The choice will affect both humans and other species.
2. A new relationship will provide benefits to both the U.S. and India.
3. The disease can be passed to both animals and people.

Unit 3 | Arts

Practice 1

Target iBT TOEFL Questions

1. Ⓑ   2. Ⓐ

iBT TOEFL Vocabulary

1. achieve   2. transition   3. innovative
4. interact   5. acclaim   6. inspire

Wrap Up

A

1. innovative   2. transition   3. inspired
4. achieved   5. acclaim   6. interact

B

1. F   2. F   3. T   4. T   5. T

Practice 2

Target iBT TOEFL Questions

1. Ⓑ   2. Ⓐ

iBT TOEFL Vocabulary

1. originate   2. consequence
3. religious   4. root
5. recognize   6. convincing

Wrap Up

A
1. roots
2. originated
3. Religious
4. convincing
5. consequences
6. recognized

B
1. T 2. F 3. F 4. T 5. T 6. F

Test 1   Orchestras
1. Ⓐ 2. Ⓑ 3. Ⓓ 4. Ⓒ 5. Ⓒ
6. Ⓓ 7. Ⓐ

Test 2   Picasso
1. Ⓒ 2. Ⓓ 3. Ⓐ 4. Ⓒ 5. Ⓒ
6. Ⓐ

Reading Helper

A
1. how to survive
2. how to speak
3. how to raise

B
1. Freshwater is important **in that** it allows many species to survive.
2. The book is valuable **in that** it gives basic explanations about the topics.
3. Plants are different from animals **in that** they get their nutrients from the Sun.

Unit 4 | Psychology

Practice 1

Target iBT TOEFL Questions
1. Ⓐ 2. Ⓑ

iBT TOEFL Vocabulary
1. fatal 2. forgetful 3. recall
4. noticeable 5. exact

Wrap Up
A
1. noticeable 2. forgetful 3. fatal
4. recall 5. exact

B
brain, language, write, aggressive, home, genetics, diet, viruses

Practice 2

Target iBT TOEFL Questions
1. Ⓒ 2. Ⓐ

iBT TOEFL Vocabulary
1. period 2. awaken
3. slow 4. shallow
5. temporarily 6. paralyze

Wrap Up
A
1. slowed 2. shallow
3. period 4. awakened
5. temporarily 6. paralyze

B
110, slowly, stops, deep, slow, rapid, increases

Test 1   Animal Assisted Therapy
1. Ⓒ 2. Ⓓ 3. Ⓑ 4. Ⓒ 5. Ⓓ
6. Ⓒ 7. Ⓑ

Test 2   Birth Order and Personality
1. Ⓒ 2. Ⓒ 3. Ⓐ 4. Ⓑ 5. Ⓒ
6. Ⓑ 7. First-born children: Ⓐ, Ⓒ, Ⓓ
Second-born children: Ⓑ, Ⓔ

Reading Helper

1. A sense of humor `has an effect on` our health.
2. Paris `is known as` the international capital of fashion.
3. Playing sports `provides` people with an opportunity to develop social skills.
4. Astronauts `have trouble` walking when they return to Earth.

Unit 5 | History

Practice 1

Target iBT TOEFL Questions

1. Ⓐ   2. Ⓐ

iBT TOEFL Vocabulary

1. contact
2. belief
3. replace
4. promote
5. concentrate
6. controversial

Wrap Up

Ⓐ
1. replaced
2. contact
3. promote
4. belief
5. concentrate
6. controversial

Ⓑ
1. (D)   2. (E)

Practice 2

Target iBT TOEFL Questions

1. Ⓒ   2. Ⓐ

iBT TOEFL Vocabulary

1. expansion   2. profit   3. earn

4. require   5. majority

Wrap Up

Ⓐ
1. expansion   2. profits
3. majority   4. earn
5. required

Ⓑ
1. T   2. F   3. T   4. F   5. T

Test 1 | Roman Slaves

1. Ⓑ   2. Ⓐ   3. Ⓒ   4. Ⓑ   5. Ⓓ
6. Ⓑ   7. Ⓓ   8. Ⓒ

Test 2 | The Paleolithic Age

1. Ⓓ   2. Ⓒ   3. Ⓓ   4. Ⓐ   5. Ⓓ
6. Ⓑ   7. Ⓐ

Reading Helper

A

1. An astronaut is a person `who is trained to travel in a spacecraft`.
2. The people `who want to succeed in the workplace` should like challenges.
3. True friends are the ones `who can give you advice`.
4. Anyone `who can solve the problem` will win the prize.

B

1. Sound is interpreted as either music <u>or</u> noise depending on the listener.
2. On the Internet, one can find many useful materials either for teaching or for <u>learning</u>.
3. Technology can be <u>either</u> good or bad depending on how it's used.

| Unit 6 | Biology |

Practice 1

Target iBT TOEFL Questions
1. Ⓒ   2. Ⓗ

iBT TOEFL Vocabulary
1. prehistoric   2. evolution
3. debate   4. highly
5. migrate

Wrap Up
A
1. migrate   2. highly
3. debate   4. prehistoric
5. evolution

B
Early Birds: (B), (C), (E)
Modern Birds: (A), (D)

Practice 2

Target iBT TOEFL Questions
1. Ⓑ   2. Ⓗ

iBT TOEFL Vocabulary
1. organism   2. function
3. release   4. vital
5. divide   6. descend

Wrap Up
A
1. vital   2. organisms
3. function   4. release
5. divided   6. descended

B
1. T   2. F   3. T   4. F   5. T

Test 1 Ants and Pheromones
1. Ⓓ   2. Ⓐ   3. Ⓐ   4. Ⓓ   5. Ⓒ
6. Ⓑ   7. Ⓓ   8. Ⓓ

Test 2 Butterfly Biodiversity
1. Ⓐ   2. Ⓓ   3. Ⓒ   4. Ⓒ   5. Ⓑ
6. Ⓑ   7. Ⓐ

Reading Helper

A
1. It wasn't clear whether the survey was performed in person or over the phone.
2. The new online service shows whether a book is in the library or checked out by someone.

B
1. (B)   2. (A)

C
1. **It was not until** the 15th century **that** it became possible to produce books quickly.
2. **It was not until** the 20th century **that** the PhD was offered for the first time.

| Unit 7 | Sociology |

Practice 1

Target iBT TOEFL Questions
Expressive Leaders: Ⓑ, Ⓓ, Ⓖ
Instrumental Leaders: Ⓒ, Ⓕ

iBT TOEFL Vocabulary
1. distant   2. order   3. discipline
4. sympathy   5. offer

Wrap Up

A
1. distant 2. discipline 3. offer
4. sympathy 5. orders

B
close → distant, advice → orders,
financial → emotional, leaders → members

Practice 2

Target iBT TOEFL Questions
After the Revolution: Ⓐ, Ⓒ, Ⓖ
Before the Revolution: Ⓔ, Ⓕ

iBT TOEFL Vocabulary
1. revolution 2. goods 3. regulate
4. purchase 5. operate

Wrap Up

A
1. operated 2. goods 3. purchase
4. revolution 5. regulate

B
hand, factories, rural, children

Test 1   Types of Society
1. Ⓐ 2. Ⓑ 3. Ⓓ 4. Ⓐ 5. Ⓒ
6. Ⓓ 7. State-organized Societies: Ⓔ,
Ⓕ, Ⓖ Pres-state Societies: Ⓐ, Ⓓ

Test 2   Surveys
1. Ⓓ 2. Ⓒ 3. Ⓐ 4. Ⓑ 5. Ⓓ
6. Ⓖ 7. Ⓓ 8. Ⓒ
9. Questionnaires: Ⓑ, Ⓔ, Ⓖ
Oral Interviews: Ⓐ, Ⓒ

Reading Helper

A
1. **While** some people support the environment, others destroy it.
2. **While** the quality of life decreases, air pollution increases.

B, C
1. The information allowed people <u>to understand</u> complicated facts more easily.
2. The project enabled the students <u>to try</u> various strategies.
3. The website will enable consumers <u>to compare</u> the prices of the products.
4. Mild weather allowed <u>the birds to stay</u> in this area.

Unit 8 | Geology

Practice 1

Target iBT TOEFL Questions
1. Ⓐ, Ⓑ, Ⓔ

iBT TOEFL Vocabulary
1. component 2. maintain
3. essentially 4. carnivore
5. herbivore 6. omnivore

Wrap Up

1. component 2. carnivores
3. Herbivores 4. Omnivores
5. essentially 6. maintain

B
① producers ② herbivores
③ carnivores ④ decomposers

Answer Keys •• 7

Practice 2

Target iBT TOEFL Questions
1. Ⓐ, Ⓔ, Ⓕ

iBT TOEFL Vocabulary
1. valuable
2. region
3. approximately
4. vast
5. occasionally
6. potentially

Wrap Up
Ⓐ
1. approximately
2. a region
3. vast
4. valuable
5. occasionally
6. potentially

Ⓑ
1. F 2. T 3. F 4. T 5. F

Test 1 Volcanoes
1. Ⓐ 2. Ⓐ 3. Ⓓ 4. Ⓓ 5. Ⓒ
6. Ⓒ 7. Ⓐ, Ⓑ, Ⓒ

Test 2 Fossils
1. Ⓓ 2. Ⓐ 3. Ⓐ 4. Ⓒ 5. Ⓐ
6. Ⓒ 7. Ⓐ 8. Ⓓ 9. Ⓐ, Ⓒ, Ⓓ

Reading Helper

Ⓐ
1. Bears eat a large amount food **before** they go into hibernation.
2. It takes time for astronauts to feel comfortable with standing **after** they return to Earth.
3. People carry the virus in their bodies for many weeks **before** the disease develops.

Ⓑ
1. The company developed a new system **which** allows users to access information more easily.
2. An ant nest has one female ant **which** lays eggs.
3. The features are grouped into categories **which** have smaller categories.

•• Actual Test

Passage 1 Lascaux Cave Paintings
1. Ⓐ 2. Ⓓ 3. Ⓐ 4. Ⓑ 5. Ⓒ
6. Ⓒ 7. Ⓑ 8. Ⓑ 9. Ⓐ, Ⓓ, Ⓔ

Passage 2 How Language Is Created
1. Ⓐ 2. Ⓐ 3. Ⓓ 4. Ⓑ 5. Ⓒ
6. Ⓒ 7. Ⓒ 8. Acronym: Ⓐ, Ⓒ, Ⓖ
Blending: Ⓔ, Ⓕ

Passage 3 IQ vs. EQ
1. Ⓑ 2. Ⓓ 3. Ⓐ 4. Ⓒ 5. Ⓐ
6. Ⓒ 7. Ⓑ 8. EQ: Ⓑ, Ⓓ, Ⓔ
IQ: Ⓐ, Ⓖ

Passage 4 Acid Rain
1. Ⓒ 2. Ⓒ 3. Ⓑ 4. Ⓑ 5. Ⓐ
6. Ⓒ 7. Ⓐ 8. Ⓓ 9. Ⓑ, Ⓓ, Ⓔ

Passage 5 Urbanization
1. Ⓒ 2. Ⓑ 3. Ⓐ 4. Ⓑ 5. Ⓓ
6. Ⓓ 7. Ⓓ 8. Ⓐ, Ⓒ, Ⓕ

Winning TOEFL iBT

PAGODA LANGUAGE EDUCATION CENTER

Reading Step 2

Step 1 • Step 2 • Step 3

Wit & Wisdom

Copyright © 2009 by PAGODA Books

All rights reserved. No part of this publication may be reproduced, stored in a retrieval system, or transmitted, in any form, or by any means, electronic, mechanical, photocopying, recording or otherwise, without the prior written permission of the copyright holder and the publisher.

Published by PAGODA Books
PAGODA Books is the professional language publishing company of the **PAGODA** Education Group.
19F, PAGODA Tower, 419, Gangnam-daero,
Seocho-gu, Seoul, 06614, Rep. of KOREA
www.pagodabook.com

Imprint | **PAGODA Books**

First published 2009
Twentieth impression 2024
Printed in the Republic of Korea

ISBN 978-89-6281-058-5 (13740)

Publisher | Kyung-Sil Park
Writer | PAGODA Language Education Center

A defective book may be exchanged at the store where you purchased it.

Winning TOEFL iBT

Reading Step 2

Wit & Wisdom

WINNING TOEFL READING

Introduction to iBT TOEFL

iBT TOEFL (internet-based TOEFL) is designed to measure how well non-native speakers of English read, listen, speak, and write in English. The test has four sections: reading, listening, speaking, and writing. Each section of the test is worth 30 points and the highest possible score on the iBT is 120 points (30 points x 4 sections). Most questions are worth 1 point each, but some of the questions in each section are worth more than 2 points.

 → **For more information, visit the ETS website (www.ets.org).**

Reading Section

(1) About the passages

In the reading section, test takers will be asked to read 3 or 5 passages. Each passage consists of 600~700 words. The test time differs according to the number of the passages given.

Number of Passages	Part & Passages			Test Time
3	Part I 1 Passage	Part II 2 Passages		60 min
5	Part I 1 Passage	Part II 2 Passages	Part III 2 Passages	100 min

The passage types are:

- Exposition: a type of writing that gives information about a topic
- Argumentation: a type of writing that develops a topic in a persuasive or logical way
- Narrative: a type of writing that describes a historical or biographical event

(2) About the questions

Each passage includes 12~14 questions. The questions test a student's ability in the following areas:

- Basic comprehension: understanding vocabulary, pronoun usage, identifying true or false information
- Reading to Learn: recognizing sentence structure, summarizing
- Inferencing: implying, recognizing the writer's purpose

To test these areas, 10 question types are used in the iBT TOEFL reading section.

Question Type	Explanation	Number of Questions	Related Unit
Basic Comprehension			
Vocabulary	Choose the word that is closest in meaning to the word that appears in the passage.	4~5	Unit 1
Pronoun	Identify the word to which a pronoun is referring.	0~1	Unit 1
True Information	Choose a sentence that is true according to the passage.	2~4	Unit 2
False Information	Choose a sentence that is NOT provided or NOT true according to the passage.	1	Unit 2
Sentence Simplification	Choose a sentence which is closest in meaning to the sentence that appears in the context.	1	Unit 3
Inferencing			
Inference	Draw an inference from the passage by choosing an answer that is not actually stated in the passage but is implied or can be inferred.	0~1	Unit 4
Rhetorical Purpose	Identify why the author has mentioned something in a certain way.	2	Unit 5
Insert text	Insert a sentence into the most appropriate place in the passage.	1	Unit 6
Reading to Learn			
Categorization	Categorize related information from the passage.	0~1	Unit 7
Summary	Choose the sentences that best summarize the entire passage.	0~1	Unit 8
Total		12~14	Actual Test

Winning TOEFL Reading Series

This is the second reading book in the *Winning TOEFL* series. It has eight units and each unit includes four passages. This book is for students who are at the beginner level, so the passages are shorter (250 words on average) and easier than the original passages seen on the actual TOEFL.

Each unit consists of:

Introduction ➜ Practice 1, 2 ➜ Test 1, 2

Each section has the following subsections.

Introduction

(1) Search! Search!

Students are encouraged to find some information about the topics on the cover page of each unit using the Internet. This part will give students the opportunity to become familiar with the topics before they actually read the passages in the Practice and Test sections of each unit.

(2) Target iBT TOEFL questions

This part introduces one or two of the iBT TOEFL question types. Each unit focuses on the following iBT TOEFL question types:

Unit 1	Vocabulary Questions Pronoun Questions
Unit 2	Finding True Information Questions Finding False information Questions
Unit 3	Sentence Simplification Questions
Unit 4	Inference Questions
Unit 5	Rhetorical Purpose Questions
Unit 6	Insert Text Questions
Unit 7	Categorization Questions
Unit 8	Summary Questions

The question types introduced in this part will be practiced repetitively in the following subsections of each unit.

Practice 1, 2

(1) Warm Up
This part functions as a pre-reading activity. Students are required to reflect on their prior knowledge of the topic by answering the questions. They are also asked to guess what the passage is about using the words on the list. This section will help students practice essential pre-reading skills such as *skimming* and *scanning*.

(2) Read the passage
This section provides a passage (about 250 words) for reading. Students are encouraged to reduce their reading time by keeping track of it.

(3) Target iBT TOEFL Questions
In this part, students can practice the target question types that they were introduced to at the beginning of each unit.

(4) iBT TOEFL Vocabulary
This section lists essential expressions that appear in the reading passage. Students are asked to match the target words with their correct meanings.

(5) Wrap Up
In this section, students can review the expressions introduced in the iBT TOEFL Vocabulary section. This section also provides a summary (note) of the passage of each practice. Students can check their overall understanding of the passage by figuring out the main ideas and the organization of the passage.

Test 1, 2

This section introduces two passages that include various kinds of iBT TOEFL questions. Students can check their comprehension with these questions.

Following Unit 8, an actual test is provided.

Actual Test

Five passages are provided as an actual test. Students will be able to check their overall understanding of many iBT TOEFL questions that they were introduced to in the previous units. The test passages contain more expressions and are slightly more difficult than the passages in each unit.

WINNING TOEFL READING

Contents

•• **Introduction** to iBT TOEFL   4
•• **Winning TOEFL Reading** Series   6

Unit 1	Language	10
Unit 2	Agriculture	26
Unit 3	Arts	42
Unit 4	Psychology	58
Unit 5	History	74
Unit 6	Biology	90
Unit 7	Sociology	106
Unit 8	Geology	122

•• **Actual Test**   138

Passage 1	Lascaux Cave Paintings	140
Passage 2	How Language Is Created	143
Passage 3	IQ vs. EQ	146
Passage 4	Acid Rain	149
Passage 5	Urbanization	153

•• **Answer Keys**
•• **MP3 files** ➔ www.pagodabook.com

UNIT 01 Language

•• Search! Search!

Find out about the topics using the Internet.
The History of Writing, Language Learning, Human Language, Artificial Language

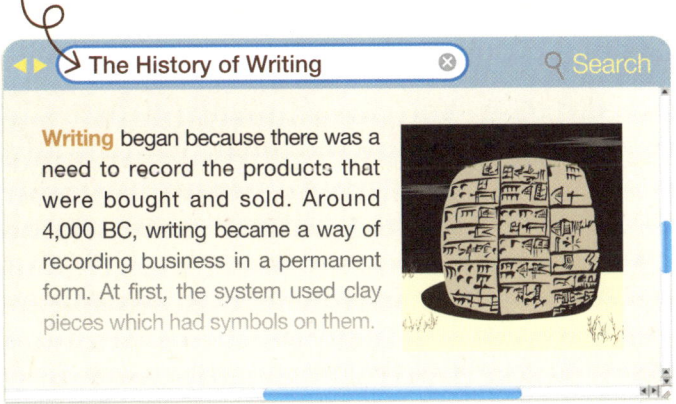

•• Target iBT TOEFL Questions

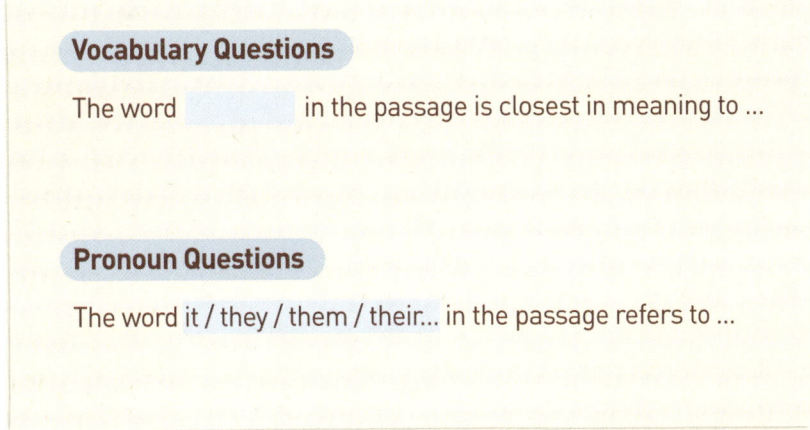

Practice 1

Warm Up

1. A baby's first word is usually the one that is the easiest to pronounce. What is most likely to be a baby's first word in an English speaking country? Choose one from the list.

   - mama
   - father
   - banana
   - piano
   - mother

Read the Passage

Your time (1st):   min, (2nd):   min

Language Learning

How do babies learn to speak? Babies pay attention to the speech they hear around them, before they can speak. Young babies respond to the sound of the human voice differently to other sounds. They will stop crying when they hear a person talking, but not if they hear a bell. Very soon, the differences in adults' voices can influence babies' emotions. Long before they can understand language, babies can sense when an adult is playful or angry. By twelve months old, babies can produce single words such as mommy or daddy. Then, they may copy short phrases. They also learn to use the same words or phrases for different purposes. For instance, "Mommy drink" might mean "Mommy is drinking" or "Mommy, I want your drink." At around age three, many toddlers speak in complete sentences.

Adults also exaggerate their speech so that babies can pick up a language easily. This is often called "baby talk". Baby talk is different from the way adults speak to each other. For example, when mothers talk to babies, they speak louder and slower. Mothers also use short, simple words or sentences with a high pitched, soft tone of voice. Baby talk is more effective than normal speech to get a baby's attention. Studies have shown that babies prefer to listen to baby talk.

Target iBT TOEFL Questions

1 The word **influence** in the passage is closest in meaning to
  Ⓐ affect   Ⓑ encourage   Ⓒ touch

2 The word **sense** in the passage is closest in meaning to
  Ⓐ observe   Ⓑ feel   Ⓒ remember

3 The word **purposes** in the passage is closest in meaning to
  Ⓐ ideas   Ⓑ reasons   Ⓒ conditions

4 The word **they** in the passage refers to
  Ⓐ adults   Ⓑ mothers   Ⓒ babies

iBT TOEFL Vocabulary

Fill in the blanks with the appropriate words.

1 _____	**v**	to react, to reply
2 _____	**v**	to imitate, to do something the way others do
3 _____	**adj**	full, including all details
4 _____	**v**	to overstate, to show as greater than is true
5 _____	**n**	a young child

- respond
- complete
- toddler
- exaggerate
- copy

Language •• 13

Wrap Up

A Complete the sentences with the appropriate words.

- copying
- responded
- exaggerate
- complete
- toddler

1 The campaign tends to _____ the negative effects of secondhand smoke.

2 A _____ is a young child between the ages of one to three years old.

3 The company _____ quickly to the customer's complaints.

4 Children learn by _____ adults' behavior.

5 The story was finally presented in its _____ form.

B Paragraph 1: Number the sentences in the correct order.
Paragraph 2: Fill in the blanks with the appropriate words.

> Paragraph 1: How do babies learn to speak?
>
> | ① | Babies pay attention to the speech they hear around them. |
> | | Babies copy short phrases. |
> | | Babies speak in complete sentences. |
> | | The differences in adults' voices influence babies' emotions. |
> | | Babies can produce single words. |
>
> Paragraph 2: Baby talk
>
> Adults _____ their speech: They speak and slower using short, simple words or sentences with a _____, soft tone of voice. Baby talk may help a child pick up a language quickly.

Practice 2

Warm Up

1 Do you think animals communicate with each other?

2 What are the differences between human language and animal communication?

Read the Passage

Human Language

Honeybees dance in order to exchange information about the location of food. Dolphins communicate using sounds like whistles. Does this mean that animals communicate with each other like humans do? There are actually large differences between human language and animal communication.

The signs used in animal communication are inborn. This means that animals can develop their signs even if they are raised away from adults of their own species. On the other hand, human language is definitely not inborn. Humans must learn language culturally, by watching and copying other humans. It must be developed over time.

In animal communication, each signal has only one function. More than one sign cannot have the same meaning. For example, gorillas have three different signals to communicate information about danger, food, and reproduction. In contrast, words in human language can mean several things.

Animal communication is not used in creative ways. Animals have a small amount of signs. Only a few messages can be expressed with a limited amount of signs. On the other hand, human language is creative. It can be used to create stories or to hide the truth. Humans can also create an unlimited number of words and sentences. New words are regularly created in societies to express trends. It is clear that animal communication is not as complex or expressive as human language.

Target iBT TOEFL Questions

1 The word **inborn** in the passage is closest in meaning to
   Ⓐ similar   Ⓑ creative   Ⓒ instinctive

2 The word **their** in the passage refers to
   Ⓐ animals   Ⓑ adults   Ⓒ species

3 The word **definitely** in the passage is closest in meaning to
   Ⓐ highly   Ⓑ clearly   Ⓒ basically

4 The word **It** in the passage refers to
   Ⓐ animal communication   Ⓑ human language   Ⓒ signal

iBT TOEFL Vocabulary

Fill in the blanks with the appropriate words.

1	**n**	a place, a point in space
2	**adj**	present at birth, instinctive
3	**v**	to grow, to take care of children until they are grown up
4	**adv**	without question or doubt
5	**adj**	not allowed to go above a certain number
6	**adv**	with constant frequency

- inborn
- definitely
- regularly
- location
- limited
- raise

Wrap Up

A Complete the sentences with the appropriate words.

- raised
- regularly
- inborn
- location
- definitely
- limited

1. At birth, babies have a/an _____ ability to grasp objects.
2. Bees that are returning to the hive dance to indicate the _____ of food.
3. Some say children must be _____ in a large family.
4. The problems are _____ not over.
5. Only a/an _____ number of people are allowed to attend the conference.
6. All of the products are checked _____ every week.

B Fill in the blanks with the sentences (a)~(d) to complete the summary note of the passage <Human Language>.

The differences between human language and animal communication:

1. Animals: The signs used in animal communication are inborn.
   Humans:
2. Animals: Each signal has only one function.
   Humans:
3. Animals: Animal communication is not used in creative ways.
   Humans:

(a) Human language can be used to create stories or hide the truth.
(b) Words in human language can mean several things.
(c) Humans learn language culturally by copying other humans.
(d) Human language creates an unlimited number of words and sentences.

The History of Writing

<An Example of Cuneiform>

In ancient times, humans lived in small tribes. At first, they traded within their own tribes. Originally, trading was verbal and only recorded using memory. However, the tribes became bigger and a lot of products began to be traded between tribes. People could no longer rely on their memory and verbal trading.

Writing began because there was a need to record the products that were bought and sold. Around 4,000 BC, writing became a way of recording business in a permanent form. At first, the system used clay pieces which had symbols on them. The symbols were displayed in vertical rows. The system used to make the markings on the pieces of clay was called cuneiform.

At first, cuneiform was used for practical and academic purposes. Cuneiform does not look like modern writing. It only involved symbols made from lines. These soon developed into wedge-shaped markings. At last, cuneiform became more detailed. [■A] It began to show language in a visual form. [■B] The written language changed as it spread to more cultures. [■C] One change was that it began to be written in horizontal rows from left to right. [■D]

Over time, cuneiform became an outdated system. Although new writing systems soon replaced it, cuneiform was the foundation for writing systems. By understanding cuneiform, we can see the growth of the first written language and of an ancient society.

* tribe: a group of people related by blood
* permanent: lasting without change

1 The word them in the passage refers to

   Ⓐ products
   Ⓑ clay pieces
   Ⓒ symbols
   Ⓓ markings

2 The word displayed in the passage is closest in meaning to

   Ⓐ used
   Ⓑ signaled
   Ⓒ shown
   Ⓓ expressed

3 According to paragraphs 1 and 2, which of the following is true of cuneiform?

   Ⓐ It began due to the need in business.
   Ⓑ It spread to small tribes.
   Ⓒ It was written from right to left.
   Ⓓ It refers to the symbols on pieces of wood.

4 The word detailed in the passage is closest in meaning to

   Ⓐ clear
   Ⓑ difficult
   Ⓒ complex
   Ⓓ popular

5 The word it in the passage refers to

   Ⓐ system
   Ⓑ cuneiform
   Ⓒ language
   Ⓓ change

6 Look at the four squares [■] that indicate where the following sentence could be added to the passage.

Soon, cuneiform spread to other cultures.

Where would the sentence best fit?

7 Which of the following best expresses the essential information in the highlighted sentence in the passage? Incorrect answer choices change the meaning in important ways or leave out essential information.

By understanding cuneiform, we can see the growth of the first written language and of an ancient society.

Ⓐ Cuneiform shows an ancient language and society.
Ⓑ Knowing about cuneiform allows us to know more about how writing and an ancient society developed.
Ⓒ Studying the first written language let us understand how cuneiform developed.
Ⓓ The development of an ancient society is closely related to the first written language.

More to know	**The Forms of Cuneiform**				
	MEANING	3,500 BC	2,500 BC	700 BC	500 BC
1	The sun	◇	✧	≩Υ	≩Υ
2	Mountain	≶<	≶<	⋉	⋉

- The forms of cuneiform underwent many changes as time passed. The marks originally looked like the shape of the object itself, but later it became more abstract through repeated use over time.

Artificial Language

Can a language be created? In 1887, a Polish doctor invented a language named Esperanto. When he was at school, he thought Latin was very difficult to learn. Later he became interested in developing a new language. He thought the language should be easy to learn. For example, every letter in Esperanto has just one sound. The grammar has only 16 rules, and all of the verbs are regular. This means that many people can learn Esperanto quite easily, even after studying for a few months. Remember that it would usually take several years to learn a second language!

A language such as Esperanto is called an artificial language. This is because the language is created for a purpose. [■A] People create artificial languages for a variety of reasons. [■B] Like Esperanto, an artificial language could be created to help international communication. [■C] An artificial language can also be created for use in literature. [■D] For instance, J.R.R. Tolkien, who wrote *The Lord of the Rings*, created languages to use in his books. In addition, international organizations like the United Nations could benefit from an artificial language. An easy second language would reduce the cost of translations in such an organization.

So far, more than 300 artificial languages have been created. Some are still in use, others have disappeared. Indeed, there are benefits that artificial languages provide. However, no one can be sure whether they can substitute natural languages.

1 According to paragraph 1, the Polish doctor became interested in developing a new language because
   Ⓐ he wanted to learn Latin faster
   Ⓑ he enjoyed inventing new things
   Ⓒ he thought learning a language should be easy
   Ⓓ he wanted to make a language like Latin

2 According to paragraph 1, which of the following is NOT mentioned as a feature of Esperanto?
   Ⓐ It has only 16 letters.
   Ⓑ The grammar has a small number of rules.
   Ⓒ All of the verbs are regular.
   Ⓓ Each letter represents only one sound.

3 Why does the author say, Remember that it would usually take several years to learn a second language! ?
   Ⓐ To show the language learner's preference to Esperanto
   Ⓑ To emphasize that Esperanto is relatively easy to learn
   Ⓒ To say that learning a language is not easy
   Ⓓ To note how long it takes to learn a second language

4 Look at the four squares [■] that indicate where the following sentence could be added to the passage.

   Tourists, businessmen, and researchers would benefit from a language that is easy to learn.

   Where would the sentence best fit?

5 The word reduce in the passage is closest in meaning to
   Ⓐ own
   Ⓑ observe
   Ⓒ approve
   Ⓓ lower

6 According to paragraph 2, all of the following are mentioned as a purpose of artificial language EXCEPT

Ⓐ literature
Ⓑ international communication
Ⓒ reducing the costs of translations
Ⓓ invention

7 The word benefits in the passage is closest in meaning to

Ⓐ advantages　　Ⓑ problems　　Ⓒ ideas　　Ⓓ rules

8 The word they in the passage refers to

Ⓐ artificial languages
Ⓑ benefits
Ⓒ natural languages
Ⓓ speakers

9 The word substitute in the passage is closest in meaning to

Ⓐ help　　Ⓑ replace　　Ⓒ change　　Ⓓ emphasize

More to know　　**Esperanto**

- Esperanto does not replace anyone's language but simply serves as a second language.
- It takes much less time to learn Esperanto than any other language. (Some say four times less).
- Esperanto gives people the opportunity to meet others from around the world.

[The Flag of Esperanto]

Reading Helper

A. Like (to give examples)

> **Examples from the passage**
> - **Like** Esperanto, an artificial language could be created to help international communication.
> (Artificial Language, Line 11)

Fill in the blanks with the appropriate examples.

- Socrates   • Mozart   • Eskimos   • United Nations   • whales   • NASA

1 Like _____'s first trip to the moon, this has also provided interesting facts about the planet.

2 Like _____, the people built igloos outside their house.

3 Like the well-known philosopher, _____, the professor kept asking questions to his students so that they could eventually find the answer by themselves.

B. as ... as

> **Examples from the passage**
> - It is clear that animal communication is not **as** complex or expressive **as** human language. (Human Language, Line 18)

Complete the sentences using the *as...as* phrase and the words given.

1 Nothing is (effective, face-to-face communication).

→

2 Some animals are (emotional, human beings).

→

3 Average stars are (not, bright, the Sun).

→

UNIT 02
Agriculture

•• Search! Search!

Find out about the topics using the Internet.
DDT, Organic Food, Water Shortage, Bird Flu

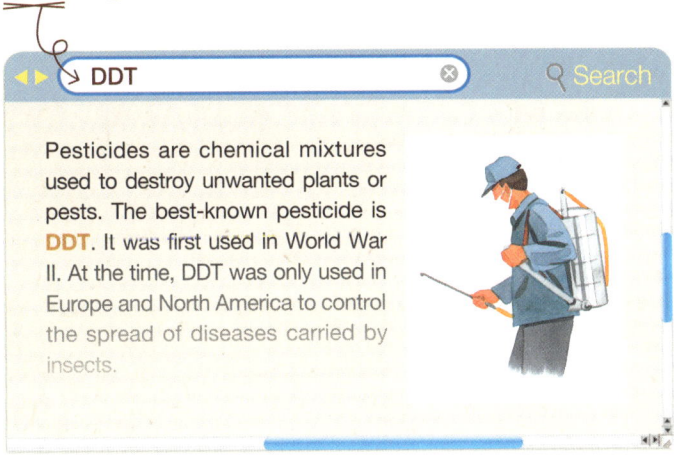

Pesticides are chemical mixtures used to destroy unwanted plants or pests. The best-known pesticide is **DDT**. It was first used in World War II. At the time, DDT was only used in Europe and North America to control the spread of diseases carried by insects.

•• Target iBT TOEFL Questions

Finding true information Questions

- According to paragraph X, which of the following is true of ...?
- According to paragraph X, A did B because ...
- According to paragraph X, A is(are) ...

Finding false information Questions

- According to paragraph X, which of the following is NOT true of ...?
- All of the following are mentioned EXCEPT ...

Practice 1

Warm Up

1 List a few of the advantages of eating organically grown foods.

- more nutrients
- _____
- _____

Read the Passage

Organic Food

Traditional farming uses chemicals to protect crops from harmful insects. It also uses <u>artificial fertilizers</u> to make plants grow. Traditional farmers give their animals hormones to make them grow faster and bigger too. These animals are usually packed into small spaces. On the other hand, organic farming only applies <u>natural fertilizers</u>. It also uses beneficial insects and birds to control harmful insects. Animals are fed organically grown feed. They are also allowed to go outside to eat the grass on the ground.

The term "Organic food" refers to foods grown and processed in an organic way. Some chemicals may be used, but the amount is carefully controlled when they are used. To be categorized as organic, more than 70 percent organic contents must be included.

Is organic food better than conventionally-grown food? Organic food can cost more than conventional food. Prices are higher because organic food is produced in small quantities. Studies about nutrition have shown mixed results. Some say that organic foods have higher nutrients than conventional food. Others say that the amount of nutrients of organic food is similar to traditional food.

Despite high prices and controversy over nutritional value, the number of organic food consumers has increased every year. Some people buy organic food to limit their exposure to chemicals. Others buy organic food for environmental reasons. They believe it lowers pollution and protects the water and soil.

* **artificial fertilizer**: chemicals that help plants grow * **natural fertilizer**: organic nutrients such as egg shells, animal bones

Target iBT TOEFL Questions

1 According to paragraph 1, which of the following is NOT true of organic farming?

Ⓐ It uses natural fertilizers.
Ⓑ It does not control harmful insects.
Ⓒ Organic animals eat grass and organic feed.

2 According to the passage, which of the following is true of organic food?

Ⓐ It must have more than 70 percent organic contents.
Ⓑ It tastes better than conventional food.
Ⓒ It is not popular due to high prices.

iBT TOEFL Vocabulary

Fill in the blanks with the appropriate words.

#	Word	Definition
1		**adj** made by people, unnatural
2		**v** to use
3		**adj** good, useful, advantageous
4		**adj** traditional, usual
5		**n** a disagreement, debate
6		**n** the state of being revealed (in danger)

- controversy
- apply
- beneficial
- exposure
- artificial
- conventional

Agriculture •• 29

Wrap Up

A Complete the sentences with the appropriate words.

- artificial
- applied
- beneficial
- conventional
- controversy
- exposure

1 The instant soup does not include any _____ flavors.
2 Drinking eight cups of water per day is _____ to one's health.
3 The _____ over the issue has grown.
4 There is a big difference between the _____ method and the new method.
5 It seems impossible to avoid _____ to viruses.
6 Most of the farmers _____ chemicals to their crops.

B Complete the summary note of the passage <Organic Food>.

Paragraph 1: _____ farming vs. Organic farming

	Traditional Farming	Organic Farming
To kill harmful insects	• uses	• uses beneficial insects and birds
To make plants grow	• uses artificial fertilizers	• uses _____ fertilizers
To make animals grow	• uses hormones	• uses organically grown feed

Paragraph 2: What is _____ food?
- Definition: foods grown and processed in an organic way
- Organic foods must include more than _____ % organic contents.

Paragraph 3: Characteristics of organic foods
- Organic food can _____ more than conventional food.
- Mixed results on nutritional value

Paragraph 4: Organic food consumers
- People buy organic foods (1) to limit their _____ to chemicals
  (2) to protect the environment

Practice 2

Warm Up

1 How do you use water? List the situations.

- To take a shower   - To brush one's teeth   - _____   - _____

2 Imagine life without water. What would happen?

Read the Passage

Your time (1st): _____ min, (2nd): _____ min

Water Shortage

Can you imagine life without water? The term "water shortage" explains the worldwide water situation in recent years. The main issue is a lack of freshwater. Freshwater includes bodies of water such as ponds, lakes, rivers and streams; the term does not include seawater. Freshwater is an important natural resource in that it allows many species to survive. It is necessary in the growth of plants. Flows of freshwater also bring nutrients and soil to the land. However, Earth has a limited amount of freshwater. Although 75% of the Earth's surface is covered by water, only 2.5% of it is freshwater. Also, 75% of all freshwater is found in glaciers and permanent snow, so it cannot be used.

People use freshwater for farming and making products. They also use freshwater to drink. As the world population grows, this demand for freshwater increases. The overuse has lowered the quantities of freshwater available. Furthermore, the industry also uses a huge amount of water. For example, more than 10,000 liters of water is used to manufacture one new car. Additionally, people remove trees in order to use the land for farming. Such tree removal has also affected the cycle of freshwater.

One study warned that two out of three people will be living without safe drinking water by 2025. The use of freshwater must be controlled before it causes more damage.

Target iBT TOEFL Questions

1 According to paragraph 1, which of the following is true of freshwater?

   Ⓐ It is found in ponds, lakes, rivers and seas.
   Ⓑ Freshwater covers 75% of the Earth's surface.
   Ⓒ 75% of freshwater is found in glaciers and permanent snow.

2 According to paragraph 2, which of the following is NOT mentioned as a cause of the water shortage?

   Ⓐ The growing population
   Ⓑ The growing ecosystem
   Ⓒ The car industry

iBT TOEFL Vocabulary

Fill in the blanks with the appropriate words.

#		Definition
1		**n** need, request
2		**n** excessive use, the use of something more than necessary
3		**v** to produce, to create
4		**v** to keep at the right limit
5		**adj** unique, specific
6		**n** a source of support or supply

- overuse
- demand
- control
- particular
- resource
- manufacture

Wrap Up

A Complete the sentences with the appropriate words.

- controlled
- resources
- manufactures
- particular
- demand
- overuse

1. The _____ for improved health care is rising.
2. The project requires _____ attention.
3. The company _____ the water pipes in India.
4. Students need to learn to use good _____.
5. The temperature in the museums is carefully _____.
6. The _____ of pesticides causes many negative effects.

B Complete the summary note of the passage <Water Shortage>.

Paragraph 1: Freshwater
- Definition: bodies of water such as ponds, lakes, _____ and streams
- Importance: (1) necessary for the growth of plants
  (2) brings _____ and soil to the land
- Amount: (1) only 2.5% of water that covers the Earth's surface
  (2) _____ % of the freshwater is found in _____ and permanent snow

Paragraph 2: _____ of freshwater shortage
(1) overpopulation → increased demand for freshwater
(2) the _____ industry   (3) tree removal

Paragraph 3: Results & Solutions
- Safe drinking water will not be available for 75% of people in the world by _____.
- The use must be controlled before it causes more damage.

Test 1

Bird Flu

Bird flu is a disease caused by bird flu viruses. Millions of birds have died from it. Moreover, tens of millions of birds have been killed to stop the disease from spreading further. Bird flu viruses are different from human flu viruses. One of the differences is that bird flu viruses naturally occur among birds. Wild birds carry the viruses in their body, but they rarely get infected by them. However, once infected, wild birds can transport the viruses to new areas. Farm birds such as chickens, ducks and turkeys are easily affected by the viruses. They can get very sick and even die.

Bird flu viruses are passed from bird to bird. The risk of humans catching bird flu is low. Nevertheless, scientists say that all flu viruses are able to change and affect humans. In fact, a subtype of bird flu has already caused humans to become ill and die. Symptoms appear within 10 days of direct contact with infected birds. The symptoms include fever, cough, sore throat, or muscle aches.

Unlike the flu, there is currently no vaccine available for humans against bird flu. Studies suggest that medicines used for treating the flu will work in treating humans for bird flu. However, flu viruses can become resistant to these drugs. In fact, two of the drugs have become ineffective against bird flu. Currently, extensive studies are taking place to develop vaccines and medicines to treat humans for bird flu.

* resistant: tending to resist, immune

1 The word them in the passage refers to

Ⓐ human flu viruses
Ⓑ wild birds
Ⓒ bird flu viruses
Ⓓ farm birds

2 According to paragraph 1, which of the following is NOT true of bird flu viruses?

Ⓐ They cause farm birds to die.
Ⓑ Farm birds carry them in their bodies.
Ⓒ They usually spread from wild birds to farm birds.
Ⓓ They rarely cause wild birds to get sick.

3 Which of the following best expresses the essential information in the highlighted sentence in the passage? Incorrect answer choices change the meaning in important ways or leave out essential information.

The risk of humans catching bird flu is low.

Ⓐ The possibility of catching bird flu is not high.
Ⓑ A few people have caught bird flu.
Ⓒ Humans rarely get sick from bird flu.
Ⓓ Most people know the danger of bird flu.

4 According to paragraph 2, all of the following are mentioned as a symptom of bird flu EXCEPT

Ⓐ muscle pain
Ⓑ cough
Ⓒ fever
Ⓓ headache

5 The word develop in the passage is closest in meaning to

Ⓐ give
Ⓑ find
Ⓒ make
Ⓓ keep

6 According to paragraphs 2 and 3, the best way to currently avoid bird flu is

Ⓐ to avoid direct contact with infected birds
Ⓑ to get vaccines
Ⓒ to take medicines before catching bird flu
Ⓓ to avoid meat from chickens and turkeys

7 According to the passage, flu viruses are different from bird flu viruses in that

Ⓐ they can cause people die
Ⓑ there are vaccines available
Ⓒ they are not easily passed
Ⓓ they are able to change

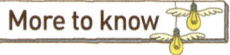 **Bird Flu Facts**

Humans might catch bird flu in the following situations:

- when they swim in infected rivers
- when they breathe air near infected birds
- when they are among infected birds
- when they play in an area where the dead bodies of infected birds are buried

DDT

Pesticides are chemical mixtures used to destroy unwanted plants or pests. The best-known pesticide is DDT. It was first used in World War II. At the time, DDT was only used in Europe and North America to control the spread of diseases carried by insects. It was very successful. In fact, the disease known as malaria was eliminated from these continents. [■A] Later, farmers began to use DDT to protect crops from insects. [■B] They found that the use of DDT meant bigger harvests and thus, more profits. [■C] In less than ten years, these positive results earned DDT worldwide fame. [■D]

However, in the 1960s, the positive attitude towards DDT began to change. During that decade, a Western biologist stated in her book that the pesticide was harming plant and animal life both on land and under water. Activists soon tried to link it to a number of other problems, including cancer in humans. All of this created a public fear of DDT, and its use became restricted. In 1972, the United States set up a ban against its use on farms. Since then, the rest of the world has done the same.

Today, the use of DDT is universally banned. The main exception is in controlling malaria-carrying mosquitoes in developing countries. Although its harmful effects are known, these countries continue to use DDT because the benefits to their societies outweigh the risks.

* **pest:** a harmful insect

1 Look at the four squares [■] that indicate where the following sentence could be added to the passage.

Indeed, the scientist who developed DDT was awarded the Nobel Prize in 1948.

Where would the sentence best fit?

2 Which of the following best expresses the essential information in the highlighted sentence in the passage? Incorrect answer choices change the meaning in important ways or leave out essential information.

They found that the use of DDT meant bigger harvests and thus, more profits.

   Ⓐ DDT helped farmers yield larger crops and earn more money.
   Ⓑ DDT saved farmers' money by protecting crops from pests.
   Ⓒ The use of DDT helped produce more crops.
   Ⓓ Farmers could save money by using DDT.

3 The word fame in the passage is closest in meaning to
   Ⓐ honor
   Ⓑ curiosity
   Ⓒ popularity
   Ⓓ value

4 According to paragraph 1, which of the following is NOT true of DDT?
   Ⓐ It has been used since World War II.
   Ⓑ The use of DDT helped farmers earn more money.
   Ⓒ Farmers developed DDT to protect crops from harmful insects.
   Ⓓ It was used to stop the spread of malaria in Europe and North America.

5 According to paragraph 1, it can be inferred that
   Ⓐ DDT was effective in many ways
   Ⓑ the use of DDT was limited to farming
   Ⓒ the harmful effects of DDT in farming were well-known
   Ⓓ it was expensive to use DDT in farming

6 The word restricted in the passage is closest in meaning to

Ⓐ limited
Ⓑ recovered
Ⓒ highlighted
Ⓓ necessary

7 The word its in the passage refers to

Ⓐ DDT
Ⓑ exception
Ⓒ control
Ⓓ malaria

8 According to paragraph 3, some countries still use DDT because

Ⓐ it is cheaper than other pesticides
Ⓑ the benefits are greater than the risks
Ⓒ there is no proof that DDT harms humans
Ⓓ it helps people become healthier

More to know **DDT Facts**

- DDT causes the thinning of eggshells.
- DDT reduces fertility in human beings.
- DDT changes the amount of activity in gold fish.
- DDT produces a massive IQ loss in children.
- DDT delays development in infants.

Reading Helper

A. Such as (to give examples)

> **Examples from the passage**
> - Freshwater includes bodies of water **such as** ponds, lakes, rivers and streams; the term does not include seawater. (Water Shortage, Line 3)
> - Farm birds **such as** chickens, ducks and turkeys are easily affected by the viruses. (Bird Flu, Line 6)

Rearrange the words in the parentheses to complete the sentences.

1 High-fiber foods (take longer / such as / beans and vegetables / to digest).

→

2 The file includes (purposes and strategies / the details of / the plan / such as).

→

3 People are starting to look at (alternative energy / solar or wind power / such as).

→

B. both... and...

Examples from the passage
- During that decade, a Western biologist stated in her book that the pesticide was harming plant and animal life **both** on land **and** under water. (DDT, Line 10)

Rearrange the words in the parentheses to complete the sentences.

1 The choice will (affect / other species / and / humans / both).

→

2 A new relationship will (and / India / benefits / provide / both / to / the U.S.).

→

3 The disease can be passed (animals / and / people / both / to).

→

UNIT 03
Arts

•• Search! Search!

Find out about the topics using the Internet.
Ancient Greek Theater, Loie Fuller, Orchestras, Picasso

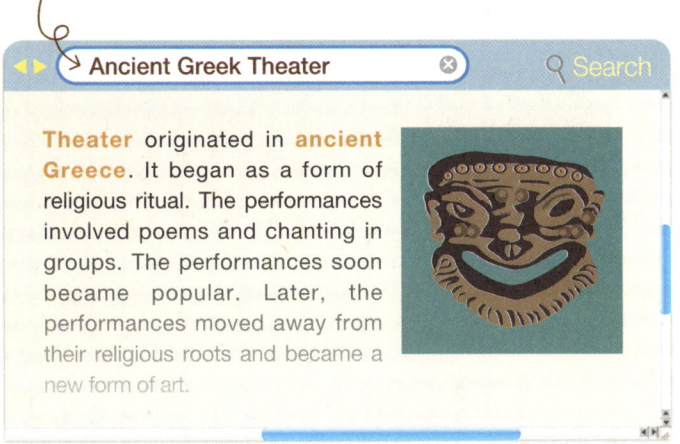

Ancient Greek Theater

Theater originated in **ancient Greece**. It began as a form of religious ritual. The performances involved poems and chanting in groups. The performances soon became popular. Later, the performances moved away from their religious roots and became a new form of art.

•• Target iBT TOEFL Questions

Sentence Simplification Questions

Which of the following best expresses the essential information in the highlighted sentence in the passage? Incorrect answer choices change the meaning in important ways or leave out essential information.

A sentence

Practice 1

Warm Up

1 List three different types of art.   ○_____   ○_____   ○_____

2 Have you ever heard of Loie Fuller? If not, who are some famous artists that you know?

Read the Passage

Your time (1st): ____ min, (2nd): ____ min

Loie Fuller

Loie Fuller was a famous American dancer in the late 1800's. She began her career by touring America with circuses. She achieved some success in America but was more successful in Europe.

Loie Fuller was born in Chicago. She began her acting career when she was 4 and made the transition to dance later. Loie was not popular as a dancer when she first started because she had been an actress first. She also didn't learn how to dance through formal lessons. Instead, she observed other performers and experimented to produce her own unique dance style.

Loie became famous for her dancing techniques and stage lighting. She created movements spontaneously while performing. Her style was innovative because she also used stage costumes that interacted with the stage lighting. Loie's innovative styles of dance and costumes in 'The Serpentine Dance' brought her great acclaim. After performing that show, she toured Europe and gained international popularity.

Although Loie died in 1928, there is still a lot of interest in her work. For example, books have been written about her life, and she has inspired art collections. There have also been lectures that discuss her dance style and her influence on other artists.

* **spontaneously:** happening at the same time

Target iBT TOEFL Questions

1. Which of the following best expresses the essential information in the highlighted sentence in the passage? Incorrect answer choices change the meaning in important ways or leave out essential information.

   Instead, she observed other performers and experimented to produce her own unique dance style.

   Ⓐ Instead of creating her own dance style, Loie learned by watching other dancers.
   Ⓑ Loie used observation and experimentation to develop a different dance style.
   Ⓒ Loie was unique because she danced by observing other dancers.

2. Which of the following best expresses the essential information in the highlighted sentence in the passage? Incorrect answer choices change the meaning in important ways or leave out essential information.

   Loie's innovative styles of dance and costumes in 'The Serpentine Dance' brought her great acclaim.

   Ⓐ Loie was praised for the new dance styles and costumes used in 'The Serpentine Dance.'
   Ⓑ 'The Serpentine Dance' was the show where Loie showed her unique style of dance and costumes.
   Ⓒ A lot of people liked Loie's innovative dance styles in 'The Serpentine Dance.'

iBT TOEFL Vocabulary

Fill in the blanks with the appropriate words.

1	**v**	to succeed, to reach the goal
2	**n**	the process of changing from one situation to another
3	**adj**	new, advanced
4	**v**	to change or affect each other
5	**n**	praise
6	**v**	to give people the enthusiasm to make something

• acclaim • innovative • interact • inspire • achieve • transition

Wrap Up

A Complete the sentences with the appropriate words.

- innovative
- interact
- inspired
- achieved
- transition
- acclaim

1 The problems of water pollution can be solved by using _____ technology.

2 It is not easy to make the _____ to a healthier lifestyle.

3 The poems have _____ a number of artists.

4 The team has _____ great success.

5 The dancer has received worldwide _____ as a performer.

6 In large groups, some students feel that they cannot _____ with their teacher.

B Check (✔) whether the sentences are True (T) or False (F) according to the passage <Loie Fuller>.

1 Loie was a famous dancer from France.   T☐   F☐

2 Loie was more popular in America than in Europe.   T☐   F☐

3 Loie was an actress before she became a dancer.   T☐   F☐

4 Loie became famous due to her innovative dance styles.   T☐   F☐

5 Loie's dance style has influenced other artists.   T☐   F☐

Practice 2

Warm Up

1 How often do you go to see plays? What is your favorite play?

Read the Passage

Your time (1st): _____ min, (2nd): _____ min

Ancient Greek Theater

<Greek Theater Mask>

Theater originated in ancient Greece. It began as a form of religious ritual. The performances involved poems and chanting in groups. The performances soon became popular. Later, the performances moved away from their religious roots and became a new form of art.

Once the performances were recognized as separate from religious ceremonies, actors were needed to play characters. Individual actors were given lines to read. The actors were always men. The men also played female characters. At the time, they also developed something called a chorus. The chorus is a group of performers who react to the actors and provide background information. The chorus also summarizes situations to help the audience understand. Sometimes, they even speak the actors' inner thoughts.

Costumes were used to display the characters. The main part of a costume was often a mask. These masks could help the male actors to be more convincing as female characters. The masks may also have helped to project the actors' voices so they could be heard in large theaters.

Ancient Greek drama focuses on tragedies. Tragedies are plays that show the lives of people who have to deal with the consequences of their actions. The main character's fault was usually arrogance, which often causes problems. Tragic performances provide lessons and examples in how to live one's life. These new performances in ancient Greece evolved into what is known as modern theater.

Target iBT TOEFL Questions

1 Which of the following best expresses the essential information in the highlighted sentence in the passage? Incorrect answer choices change the meaning in important ways or leave out essential information.

> Once the performances were recognized as separate from religious ceremonies, actors were needed to play characters.

Ⓐ During religious ceremonies, actors weren't needed to play characters.
Ⓑ Actors became necessary in order to play characters when performances separated from religious ceremonies.
Ⓒ There were no characters to play when performances were part of religious ceremonies.

2 Which of the following best expresses the essential information in the highlighted sentence in the passage? Incorrect answer choices change the meaning in important ways or leave out essential information.

> Tragedies are plays that show the lives of people who have to deal with the consequences of their actions.

Ⓐ Tragedies show examples of how people's actions can affect what happens to them later.
Ⓑ Tragedies give examples of people who behave badly and are punished for it.
Ⓒ The purpose of tragic plays is to teach people how to live their lives.

iBT TOEFL Vocabulary

Fill in the blanks with the appropriate words.

1. _____ **v** to come from, to appear for the first time
2. _____ **n** the result that is caused by previous events
3. _____ **adj** relating to religion or beliefs
4. _____ **n** origin, beginning
5. _____ **v** to be aware of
6. _____ **adj** persuasive, believable

• convincing • religious • root • recognize • originate • consequence

Wrap Up

A Complete the sentences with the appropriate words.

- recognized
- consequences
- originated
- religious
- roots
- convincing

1 Adopted children have a right to learn about their _____.

2 Yoga _____ from ancient India.

3 _____ groups can play an active role in society.

4 The research has provided a _____ explanation about the beginning of the universe.

5 The _____ of the accident were tragic.

6 The symptoms are well _____ as possible signs of Alzheimer's disease.

B Check (✔) whether the sentences are True (T) or False (F) according to the passage <Ancient Greek Theater>.

1 Theater originally began as religious rituals. T☐ F☐

2 It took time for the religious rituals to become popular. T☐ F☐

3 Performances evolved into a new form of art before they became popular. T☐ F☐

4 Ancient Greek dramas can be characterized as tragedies. T☐ F☐

5 Female characters were played by male performers. T☐ F☐

6 Female actors had to wear masks to be on stage. T☐ F☐

Arts •• 49

Test 1

Orchestras

We can learn more about the evolution of music by looking at the history of orchestras. The first known orchestras existed in ancient Egypt. They were made of small groups of musicians that gathered for festivals or holidays. During the Roman Empire, non-government musicians were banned. However, groups of instruments with different tones continued to appear.

Modern orchestras started in the late 16th century. The 17th century saw an increase in instruments with strings, such as violins. This was also a time for innovations in instrument making, music writing, and performance techniques.

In the 18th century, Richard Wagner's musical dramas were more complex and used a broad range of musical instruments. [■A] This meant they needed a conductor to direct the musicians. [■B] Wagner's work changed the way music was written for orchestras. [■C] It also influenced the writing style for the next 80 years. [■D] Orchestras in the mid-19th century had sixty players. In the early 20th century, they grew to over a hundred players for some pieces of music. Today's orchestras are made up of approximately ninety musicians.

The composer Beethoven is said to have influenced the structure of orchestras. His music usually uses a pair of wind instruments such as flutes and clarinets. Several years after Beethoven's death, most musical pieces used the same structure that he used. Nowadays, orchestras use a wider range of instruments and experiment with new sounds.

1 Which of the following best expresses the essential information in the highlighted sentence in the passage? Incorrect answer choices change the meaning in important ways or leave out essential information.

> We can learn more about the evolution of music by looking at the history of orchestras.

Ⓐ By learning how orchestras changed over time, we can understand the development of music.
Ⓑ To understand how orchestras developed, we must study the development of music.
Ⓒ It is helpful to understand the development of orchestras.
Ⓓ The changes made to orchestras over time have affected the development of all musical instruments.

2 In paragraph 1, the author mentions orchestras in the Roman Empire in the passage in order to

Ⓐ show the size of the Roman orchestras
Ⓑ provide an example of the difficulties faced in the development of music
Ⓒ mention the importance of music in the western world
Ⓓ explain a major era of orchestral development

3 Look at the four squares [■] that indicate where the following sentence could be added to the passage.

The size of orchestras has also changed over time.

Where would the sentence best fit?

4 The word they in the passage refers to

Ⓐ musical dramas　　Ⓑ musical instruments　Ⓒ orchestras　　Ⓓ players

5 The word approximately in the passage is closest in meaning to

Ⓐ totally　　　　　　Ⓑ actually　　　　　　Ⓒ nearly　　　　Ⓓ formerly

Arts • 51

6 According to paragraph 3, all of the following changed due to Wagner's influence on orchestras EXCEPT

　Ⓐ the use of musical instruments
　Ⓑ the use of a conductor
　Ⓒ the writing style
　Ⓓ the structure of orchestras

7 Which of the following best expresses the essential information in the highlighted sentence in the passage? Incorrect answer choices change the meaning in important ways or leave out essential information.

> Several years after Beethoven's death, most musical pieces used the same structure that he used.

　Ⓐ After his death, most musical pieces began to follow the structure Beethoven created.
　Ⓑ Beethoven created a structure that most musical pieces could use.
　Ⓒ When Beethoven died, his musical structure became popular among other musicians.
　Ⓓ The structure of most musical pieces today follows Beethoven's works.

 **The New York Philharmonic Orchestra**

The New York Philharmonic is the oldest symphony orchestra in the United States. It was founded in 1842 by a group of local musicians. The orchestra currently plays about 180 concerts each year. On December 18, 2004, the Philharmonic gave its 14,000th concert. Since 1917, it has recorded nearly 2,000 albums.

Test 2

Picasso

Pablo Picasso was born in Spain in 1881. His father was an art teacher. He taught Picasso how to draw and paint using oils. Picasso's work is often organized into time periods.

[■A] The Blue Period began shortly after he moved to Paris from Barcelona. [■B] In his late teens, it was his first time away from home. [■C] During this period, he had poor living conditions, and he also lost his close friend to suicide. [■D] At the time, he mostly used blue and blue-green colors. This was called the Blue Period. Most of the Blue Period paintings are considered to be emotional and depressing.

The Rose Period began in 1905. This period represents a more cheerful style, using orange and pink colors. His main subjects were circus entertainers and clowns. During the Rose Period, Picasso's paintings seemed more positive because he used brighter colors.

From 1907 to 1909, Picasso's work was influenced by African art forms, especially masks. Consequently, this period is known as the African Period. His paintings used angular forms and became simple.

The most famous of all periods was the Cubist. His paintings featured brown and other neutral colors. Picasso developed this style with another artist. The style focused the shapes of objects, rather than painting them exactly as they looked.

Towards the end of his life, Picasso used a mixture of his past styles. Picasso had always been ahead of his time in that he tried to develop new styles of painting.

1 According to paragraph 2, which of the following is NOT true of the Blue Period?
  Ⓐ Picasso's friend died.
  Ⓑ Picasso mostly used blue colors.
  Ⓒ The paintings expressed a positive view.
  Ⓓ Picasso was a teenager.

2 Look at the four squares [■] that indicate where the following sentence could be added to the passage.

Such depressing experiences were most easily seen in his use of colors.

Where would the sentence best fit?

3 Which of the following best expresses the essential information in the highlighted sentence in the passage? Incorrect answer choices change the meaning in important ways or leave out essential information.

> During the Rose Period, Picasso's paintings seemed more positive because he used brighter colors.

  Ⓐ Picasso's paintings during this period were colorful and suggested an optimistic attitude.
  Ⓑ The colors that Picasso used in this period of painting show his emotions at the time.
  Ⓒ Picasso was more optimistic during the Rose Period than the Blue Period.
  Ⓓ The use of colors during the Rose Period show Picasso's attitude toward his paintings.

4 The word exactly in the passage is closest in meaning to
  Ⓐ almost
  Ⓑ roughly
  Ⓒ perfectly
  Ⓓ mostly

5 Which of the following best expresses the essential information in the highlighted sentence in the passage? Incorrect answer choices change the meaning in important ways or leave out essential information.

> Picasso had always been ahead of his time in that he tried to develop new styles of painting.

Ⓐ Picasso's paintings brought him a lot of attention because they were so different.
Ⓑ Picasso was often misunderstood by the art world because of his strange styles of painting.
Ⓒ Picasso was innovative since he developed new styles of painting before others.
Ⓓ The painting styles that Picasso created led the rest of the art world.

6 According to the passage, which of the following is true of Picasso's painting styles?

Ⓐ He always tried to develop his own style.
Ⓑ He used brownish colors in the Rose Period.
Ⓒ His paintings had an influence on African art forms.
Ⓓ He mostly used blue colors.

More to know **Picasso's Quotes**

- "Painting is just another way of keeping a diary."
- "I paint objects as I think them, not as I see them."
- "Art is a lie that makes us realize truth."
- "Art washes away from the soul the dust of everyday life."
- "The world today doesn't make sense, so why should I paint pictures that do?"

Reading Helper

A. how to do

> **Examples from the passage**
>
> - Tragic performances provide lessons and examples in **how to live** one's life.
>   (Ancient Greek Theater, Line 20)
> - She also didn't learn **how to dance** through formal lessons. (Loie Fuller, Line 8)
> - He taught Picasso **how to draw and paint** using oils. (Picasso, Line 1)

Fill in the blanks using *how to* and the verbs in the parentheses.

1 Through their history, Native Americans figured out _____ (survive) in cold weather.

2 Babies learn _____ (speak) by imitating what they hear.

3 The new book is about _____ (raise) children.

B. in that

> **Examples from the passage**
> - Picasso had always been ahead of his time **in that** he tried to develop new styles of painting.
> (Picasso, Line 22)

Combine the two sentences using the expression *in that*.

1 Freshwater is important. Freshwater allows many species to survive.

→

2 The book is valuable. The book gives basic explanations about the topics.

→

3 Plants are different from animals. Plants get their nutrients from the Sun.

→

UNIT 04
Psychology

•• Search! Search!

Find out about the topics using the Internet.
Animal Assisted Therapy, Alzheimer's Disease,
Sleep Cycles and the Stages of Sleep, Birth Order and Personality

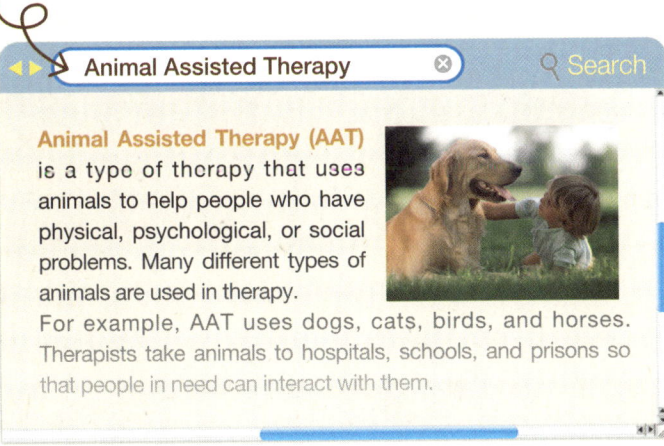

•• Target iBT TOEFL Questions

Inference Questions

- According to paragraph X, what can be inferred about _____?

- According to paragraph X, it can be inferred about _____ that...

Practice 1

Warm Up

1. The following are extremely normal situations. Check (✔) the ones you have experienced.
   - ☐ Often forgetting names
   - ☐ Temporarily misplacing bags or keys
   - ☐ Sometimes having trouble finding the right word
   - ☐ Forgetting why you came into a room

Read the Passage

Your time (1st): _____ min, (2nd): _____ min

Alzheimer's Disease

Alzheimer's is a disease that destroys brain cells. By doing this, it causes problems with memory, thinking, and language. These problems eventually affect a person's ability to work, enjoy hobbies, and carry on a social life. Sadly, Alzheimer's gets worse over time and is fatal.

In the early stages of the disease, the person might be a bit forgetful. Alzheimer's patients have trouble recalling recent events, yet they remember past events very clearly. As time passes, however, they have trouble recalling the names of people and things they once knew well. For them, simple math problems become difficult. Over time, more symptoms become noticeable. Patients forget how to do simple tasks like brushing their teeth. They have trouble speaking. They even lose the ability to read and write. In the final stages, patients can become anxious or aggressive. They often get lost on their way home. Thus, in the final stages, people with Alzheimer's need constant care.

Although there has been a lot of research, the exact causes are still unknown. It is known that age is the most important risk factor. Another risk factor is genetics. While it is rare, children of those who carry the gene have an increased chance of developing the disease between the ages of 30 and 60. Today, experts are interested in how education, diet, the environment, and viruses affect Alzheimer's.

Target iBT TOEFL Questions

1 According to paragraph 2, what can be inferred about the symptoms of Alzheimer's disease?

Ⓐ Most of the symptoms are related to memory.
Ⓑ The symptoms appear in the final stages.
Ⓒ As time passes, some of the symptoms disappear.

2 According to paragraph 3, it can be inferred about Alzheimer's disease that

Ⓐ only old people can be affected by this disease
Ⓑ experts assume that there may be many more factors that cause Alzheimer's
Ⓒ it is not likely transferred through generations

iBT TOEFL Vocabulary

Fill in the blanks with the appropriate words.

1 _____	**adj**	deadly, with very serious negative effects
2 _____	**adj**	likely to forget
3 _____	**v**	to remember something
4 _____	**adj**	easily seen
5 _____	**adj**	accurate, correct

- fatal
- noticeable
- forgetful
- recall
- exact

Psychology •• 61

Wrap Up

A Complete the sentences with the appropriate words.

- fatal
- recall
- forgetful
- noticeable
- exact

1 The improvement was _____ but not huge.

2 Old people are sometimes _____.

3 Some of the negative effects of smoking are _____.

4 Many factors can affect the ability to _____ memories.

5 Despite a lot of effort, the _____ causes of cancer are still unknown.

B Complete the summary note of the passage <Alzheimer's Disease>.

Paragraph 1: What is Alzheimer's Disease?
- destroys _____ cells
  → causes problems with memory, thinking, and _____

Paragraph 2: Symptoms
- forgetfulness
- difficulty in communication (lose the ability to speak, read, and _____)
- changes in personality (become anxious or _____)
- memory loss (getting lost on their way _____)

Paragraph 3: Possible Causes
(1) age
(2) _____
(3) education, _____, environment, _____

Practice 2

Warm Up

1 How many hours do you sleep in a day?

2 Do you dream while asleep? What do you dream of?

Read the Passage

Your time (1st): ____ min, (2nd): ____ min

Sleep Cycles and the Stages of Sleep

Most people pass through five stages when they sleep. These include the 1st, 2nd, 3rd, 4th and REM (Rapid Eye Movement) stages. These stages occur in cycles. In most cases, one complete cycle takes between 90 and 110 minutes. Early in the night, cycles have short periods of REM sleep and long periods of deep sleep. Later in the night, however, REM periods become longer and deep sleep periods become shorter.

The first stage is the drowsy stage. In this stage, a person can be awakened easily. The eyes move slowly and muscle activity slows. Brain activity decreases by 50%. The second stage is the light sleep stage. During this stage, eye movement stops and brain waves become slower. When a person enters the third stage, the brain begins to produce slow delta waves. In the fourth stage, the brain produces only delta waves. Stages 3 and 4 are known as deep sleep. It is very difficult to wake someone from these stages. In deep sleep, there is no eye movement or muscle activity.

In REM sleep, breathing becomes more rapid and shallow, eyes move quickly, and big muscles are temporarily paralyzed. Brain waves increase to the same level as when a person is awake. Also, heart rate and blood pressure rises. This is the time when most dreams occur. Most people experience three to five periods of REM sleep every night.

Target iBT TOEFL Questions

1 According to paragraph 1, what can be inferred about sleep cycles?

   Ⓐ Sleep cycles do not always include REM sleep.
   Ⓑ One complete sleep cycle includes at least four stages.
   Ⓒ The stages of sleep change throughout the night.

2 According to the passage, what can be inferred about REM sleep?

   Ⓐ The REM stage can be an ideal time for waking up.
   Ⓑ People always dream during REM sleep.
   Ⓒ The REM periods will become longer early in the morning.

iBT TOEFL Vocabulary

Fill in the blanks with the appropriate words.

#	Word	Part	Definition
1		n	an amount of time
2		v	to become awake or conscious
3		v	to become slow, to move slowly
4		adj	not deep
5		adv	for a brief or limited period of time
6		v	to be unable to move or function

- period
- temporarily
- paralyze
- awaken
- slow
- shallow

Wrap Up

A Complete the sentences with the appropriate words.

• period	• awakened	• slowed
• shallow	• temporarily	• paralyze

1 Economic growth _____ while the unemployment rate increased.
2 The lake has become _____ within the last 10 years. It will soon dry up.
3 The book was published during the _____ of Elizabeth I.
4 Bears can be _____ during their long winter sleep.
5 The national park is closed _____ due to flood damage. It will reopen next month.
6 The strikes can _____ the country.

B Correct the underlined words to complete the summary note of the passage <Sleep Cycles and the Stages of Sleep>.

Sleep Cycles

The five stages of sleep (1st, 2nd, 3rd, 4th, REM) occur in cycles. One cycle takes between 90 and <u>160 minutes</u>.

Stages of Sleep
(1) 1st (Drowsy stage): Can be easily <u>awaken</u>.
　　　　　　　　　　The eyes move <u>quickly</u> and muscle activity slows.
(2) 2nd (Light Sleep): Eye movement <u>begins</u> and brain waves become slower.
(3) 3rd (<u>Light</u> Sleep): Brain begins to produce <u>fast</u> delta waves.
(4) 4th (Deep Sleep): The brain produces only delta waves.
(5) REM: • Breathing becomes <u>slow</u> and shallow.　• Eyes move quickly.
　　　　• Heart rate and blood pressure <u>lowers</u>.　• Most dreams occur.

Animal Assisted Therapy

Animal Assisted Therapy (AAT) is a type of therapy that uses animals to help people who have physical, psychological, or social problems. Many different types of animals are used in therapy. For example, AAT uses dogs, cats, birds, and horses. Therapists take animals to hospitals, schools, and prisons so that people in need can interact with them.

AAT helps people learn life lessons. [■A] It also helps them overcome stress and injuries. [■B] An animal, like a family pet, can help a person learn family values and responsibility. [■C] At the same time, many people feel comforted when touching animals. [■D] Caring for pets also provides people with the chance to socialize with other pet owners. The use of horses is another good example of how effective AAT can be. Through therapeutic riding, people can exercise. They can build motor skills and improve balance. Moreover, being close to a horse helps improve their ability to focus.

AAT offers many benefits. First of all, it allows therapists to use a single tool, an animal, to achieve a number of goals. Physical goals increase a patient's range of motion, strength, balance, and sense of touch. Psychological goals help people overcome loneliness and depression. Finally, social goals help people build relationships and increase self-esteem. In sum, there may be no other form of therapy that offers such a wide variety of benefits.

* therapist: a person who is skilled in a particular type of therapy
* therapeutic: relating to therapy

1 The word them in the passage refers to

   Ⓐ problems
   Ⓑ therapists
   Ⓒ animals
   Ⓓ people

2 Look at the four squares [■] that indicate where the following sentence could be added to the passage.

   Studies show that petting animals helps lower blood pressure.

   Where would the sentence best fit?

3 Why does the author mention horses in paragraph 2?

   Ⓐ To show that AAT can use big animals
   Ⓑ To introduce one more advantage of AAT
   Ⓒ To explain how horses are used in AAT
   Ⓓ To explain how patients can overcome stress

4 The word effective in the passage is closest in meaning to

   Ⓐ active
   Ⓑ common
   Ⓒ excellent
   Ⓓ strong

5 According to paragraph 2, it can be inferred that AAT

   Ⓐ only uses small animals
   Ⓑ does not require any therapists
   Ⓒ is not always appropriate for every situation
   Ⓓ can be used to perform many different functions

6 According to paragraph 3, which of the following is NOT mentioned about AAT?

Ⓐ It can help people overcome emotional difficulties.

Ⓑ It can increase patients' physical strength.

Ⓒ It can improve language skills.

Ⓓ It can help people develop social skills.

7 Which of the following best expresses the essential information in the highlighted sentence in the passage? Incorrect answer choices change the meaning in important ways or leave out essential information.

==In sum, there may be no other form of therapy that offers such a wide variety of benefits.==

Ⓐ Because of its large number of benefits, AAT is a very popular kind of therapy.

Ⓑ AAT is a unique type of therapy in that it provides so many different benefits.

Ⓒ It is not easy to find therapies that can address so many different problems.

Ⓓ AAT is one of the only known therapies that can provide more than one benefit.

More to know   **Therapy Dogs vs. Service Dogs**

- **Therapy dogs** are dogs trained to provide comfort to people in hospitals, retirement homes or nursing homes. They are used to lift spirits and promote healing.

- **Service dogs** are dogs trained to help people who have disabilities in vision or hearing. They can act as the helper for people with disabilities.

Birth Order and Personality

Birth order is a person's rank by age among his or her siblings. Birth order can influence differences in personality. Birth order is also believed to have an important effect on psychological development. Although this idea has been challenged by researchers, birth order continues to attract interest.

The first child will always be "first" in the parents' lives. It is common for the first-born to resent losing the parents' attention when new siblings arrive. The oldest child will be the first to achieve things, so other children will be measured against the first-born. Because of this, first-borns often develop a sense of responsibility at an early age. Thus, first-born children commonly make good leaders.

The experience of the second-born child is also unique. [■A] For many second-born children, older and younger siblings tend to take most of the attention. [■B] These "middle" children can feel overlooked. [■C] As a result of their middle status, second-born children are often better at negotiating than their siblings. They tend to be the most independent child in the family.

Finally, the last-born child can also face difficulties. [■D] Being the "baby" of the family means being the last to do things. This can be frustrating. The third-born child often wants to do things with older siblings but feels isolated. This can lead to behavior problems. As a result, third-born children often feel angry towards their older siblings. Ultimately, it is important that all children feel valued. They need to feel that they have a special place within the family unit, regardless of birth order.

* **sibling:** one's brother or sister
* **resent:** to feel bitter about something
* **isolated:** kept away from others, left out

1 The word challenged in the passage is closest in meaning to

Ⓐ developed   Ⓑ defended   Ⓒ opposed   Ⓓ changed

2 Look at the four squares [■] that indicate where the following sentence could be added to the passage.

Therefore, middle children need to feel that they have an important place in the family.

Where would the sentence best fit?

3 The word Ultimately in the passage is closest in meaning to

Ⓐ finally   Ⓑ clearly   Ⓒ normally   Ⓓ largely

4 Which of the following best expresses the essential information in the highlighted sentence in the passage? Incorrect answer choices change the meaning in important ways or leave out essential information.

They need to feel that they have a special place within the family unit, regardless of birth order.

Ⓐ Children must be able to feel that they are special in their family.
Ⓑ No matter how they rank in age, each child should feel special within the family.
Ⓒ Children should be treated well according to their birth order.
Ⓓ The order of birth should not determine the way a child gets treated.

5 According to paragraph 4, which of the following is true of third-born children?

Ⓐ They often feel frustrated with their parents.
Ⓑ They need more attention than first and second-born children.
Ⓒ They often have difficulty getting along with older siblings.
Ⓓ They never have behavior problems.

6 According to the passage, what can be inferred about birth order?

  Ⓐ The oldest child lacks responsibility compared to his or her siblings.
  Ⓑ Each birth order rank has its own benefits and difficulties.
  Ⓒ There have been no challenges to the idea that birth order and personality are related.
  Ⓓ Parents tend to treat their children differently according to their birth order.

7 Directions: Complete the table below about the two types of birth order discussed in the passage. Match the appropriate phrases to the types of birth order with which they are associated. Two of the answer choices will NOT be used.

Answer Choices

Ⓐ resent losing parents' attention
Ⓑ tend to be independent
Ⓒ are the first to do things
Ⓓ tend to have leadership qualities
Ⓔ are good negotiators
Ⓕ feel valued
Ⓖ cause problems

First-born Children
-
-
-

Second-born Children
-
-

| More to know | **Common Positive Traits** |

- **First-born children**: energetic, ambitious, natural leaders, precise, competent
- **Middle-born children**: peace makers, get along with others, independent, competitive, realistic
- **Last-born children**: sociable, outgoing, creative, confident, good sense of humor

:: Reading Helper

A. be known as

Examples from the passage

- Stages 3 and 4 **are known as** deep sleep. (Sleep Cycles and the Stages of Sleep, Line 14)

B. have an (important) effect on

Examples from the passage

- Birth order is also believed to **have an important effect on** psychological development. (Birth Order and Personality, Line 2)

C. provide ... with

Examples from the passage

- Caring for pets also **provides** people **with** the chance to socialize with other pet owners. (Animal Assisted Therapy, Line 11)

D. have trouble ...ing

Examples from the passage

- Alzheimer's patients **have trouble** recall**ing** recent events, yet they remember past events very clearly. (Alzheimer's Disease, Line 6)
- They **have trouble** speak**ing**. (Alzheimer's Disease, Line 10)

Complete the sentences with the appropriate words. Change the form, if necessary.

- be known as
- have an effect on
- provide
- have trouble

1 A sense of humor _____ our health.

2 Paris _____ the international capital of fashion.

3 Playing sports _____ people with an opportunity to develop social skills.

4 Astronauts _____ walking when they return to Earth.

Go through the four passages in Unit 4 and find these expressions;

continue to, tend to, interact with

Write the sentences that include the expressions in the note below.

UNIT 05
History

•• Search! Search!

Find out about the topics using the Internet.
Universities, Children in the Victorian Age, Roman Slaves, The Paleolithic Age

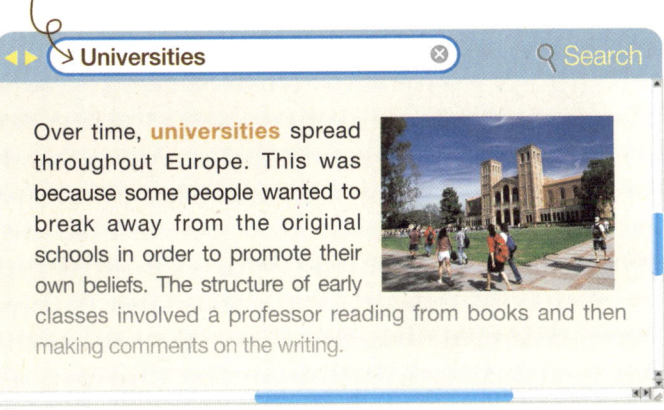

•• Target iBT TOEFL Questions

Rhetorical Purpose Questions

- The author mentions _____ in order to ...
- The author says/discusses _____ by (giving examples...)
- What's the function of paragraph X as it relates to the rest of the passage?

Practice 1

Warm Up

1 Do you know which university has the longest history in your country?

Read the Passage

Universities

Before the 12th century, education in Europe took place in cathedrals. At first, only the young men who wanted to join the church were able to learn. During the 12th century, however, this changed. At the time, the population of Europe grew. People also came into contact with knowledge from the Muslim world. The Muslims had schools and libraries full of books. Many of these contained copies of works by famous thinkers such as Socrates.

By the end of the 12th century, universities had replaced cathedrals as places of learning. At first, students gathered in towns to study under professors. They began to form guilds of students and professors. These guilds were the world's first universities. Students of these early universities could study law, medicine, and the arts. For centuries, universities were for men only. It would be a long time before women were allowed to study or teach in universities.

Over time, universities spread throughout Europe. This was because some people wanted to break away from the original schools in order to promote their own beliefs. The structure of early classes involved a professor reading from books and then making comments on the writing. At first, it was common for students to be taught by other students. Professors often asked controversial questions to encourage discussion. By the 18th century, professors began to concentrate on shaping the minds of the elite.

* **guild:** a formal group of people with similar interests

Target iBT TOEFL Questions

1 In the passage, the author explains how universities developed by

Ⓐ discussing the changes over time
Ⓑ comparing cathedrals to schools
Ⓒ showing a relationship between cathedrals and universities

2 The word grew in the passage is closest in meaning to

Ⓐ increased　　　　　　Ⓑ fell　　　　　　Ⓒ changed

iBT TOEFL Vocabulary

Fill in the blanks with the appropriate words.

1 _____ **n** a close interaction
2 _____ **n** an opinion, a feeling that something is true
3 _____ **v** to put a new person or thing in place of another
4 _____ **v** to support the growth of
5 _____ **v** to focus one's attention on something
6 _____ **adj** open to question

- belief
- controversial
- replace
- contact
- promote
- concentrate

Wrap Up

A Complete the sentences with the appropriate words.

- contact
- belief
- replaced
- promote
- controversial
- concentrate

1 Any theory can be _____ by other theories.

2 The trip provided _____ with local culture and people.

3 There are several ways to _____ children's health.

4 The _____ that intelligence can be measured by IQ test has been challenged.

5 A great way to learn is to _____ and practice a lot.

6 Online copyright is a _____ issue in many countries.

B Where would the sentences fit best in the summary of the passage <Universities>?
Write the appropriate letter next to each sentence.

1 For centuries, women were not allowed to study in universities.

2 The popularity was because many people wanted to develop their own beliefs in universities.

> Before the 12th century, cathedrals were the places of learning for young men. (A) Contact with the Muslim world changed this tradition. (B) By the end of the 12th century, students and professors formed guilds for studying. (C) The guilds were the world's first universities. (D) Over time, universities spread throughout Europe. (E) The structure of classes also changed. By the 18th century, professors began to concentrate on raising the elite people of society in universities.

Practice 2

Warm Up

1 Identify the topic and read the passage quickly. What do you think the passage is mainly about?

☐ The life of children in the Victorian Age

☐ The effect of industrial growth within England

Read the Passage

Your time (1st): _____ min, (2nd): _____ min

Children in the Victorian Age

The Victorian Age was the period during which Queen Victoria ruled England. It lasted from 1837 to 1901 and was a time of expansion. A major reason for this expansion was the industrial growth within England. Factories made profits and families grew in size. **Between 1851 and 1901, the population rose from 16.8 million to 30.5 million.** With this increase, however, working class families had to work hard to survive. In most cases, children also had to work to earn enough money for the family.

During the Victorian Age, children were sent to work at a young age. Boys worked six days a week in factories and mines. Children were used to pick up dropped tools from under machines in factories. They were also required to crawl through small tunnels in the mines. It was common for children to suffer serious injuries doing these jobs.

The growth of industry eventually led to the growth of a large and educated middle class. Yet, at the time, school was not free. Thus, only children of the rich were educated. Because most people were poor, the majority of English children were forced to go to work. This did not begin to change until 1870, when the *Education Act* was passed. It offered schools for children between the ages of five and thirteen. It was not until 1891, however, that elementary education became free for all children in England.

Target iBT TOEFL Questions

1 Why does the author mention Between 1851 and 1901, the population rose from 16.8 million to 30.5 million?

Ⓐ To provide one more reason for the expansion of England
Ⓑ To explain the causes of the industrial growth
Ⓒ To show how dramatically the population increased

2 What's the function of paragraph 1 as it relates to the rest of the passage?

Ⓐ It gives background knowledge about the Victorian Age.
Ⓑ It explains the causes of the *Education Act* mentioned in paragraph 3.
Ⓒ It highlights how the English middle class appeared in the Victorian Age.

iBT TOEFL Vocabulary

Fill in the blanks with the appropriate words.

1. _____ **n** growth, the process of increasing in size
2. _____ **n** gain, money that one makes by selling something
3. _____ **v** to receive something as a result of your efforts
4. _____ **v** to make someone do something, to ask something of someone
5. _____ **n** most of the people or things in a group

- earn
- profit
- expansion
- require
- majority

Wrap Up

A Complete the sentences with the appropriate words.

- expansion
- profits
- earn
- required
- majority

1 The industries grew through the _____ of railroads.

2 Only a limited number of companies made _____ during the economic crisis.

3 The _____ of immigrants were in their 30s.

4 Victorian children risked their lives to _____ small amounts of money in factories.

5 The students were _____ to join study groups.

B Check (✔) whether the sentences are True (T) or False (F) according to the passage <Children in the Victorian Age>.

1 Victorian children had to work in factories and mines.   T☐   F☐

2 Every Victorian child had a right to a free education.   T☐   F☐

3 Poor children often had to work six days a week.   T☐   F☐

4 The industry developed as the middle classes grew.   T☐   F☐

5 All Victorian children were able to receive elementary education for free in 1891.   T☐   F☐

Test 1

Roman Slaves

In Ancient Rome, a large number of men and women served as slaves of either the Roman government or wealthy people. In many cases, slaves were prisoners captured in war and sent back to Rome to be sold. Anyone who had enough money could buy them. Once sold, they became the property of their owners and had to work for no money. As most Roman citizens did not perform manual work, slaves did many different kinds of jobs for them. Thus, slaves formed an important part of the economy.

Most of these slaves worked on farms owned by wealthy landholders. On these farms, they were forced to work all day. Other slaves were forced to work in mines, digging gold, silver, or iron for the Roman government. The government owned many men who rowed ships as slaves. Most of these men had been sentenced to the mines or to the ships as punishment. The conditions were harsh, and these slaves often died after just a few years.

There were a lot of slaves, however, who were skilled and worked in factories or craft shops. They did things like weaving and pottery. They even made intricate mosaics. It was also common for slaves to work as house servants. [■A] This meant they were nannies, nurses, cooks, tutors for children, and even accountants. [■B] This was not always a terrible life. [■C] Many slaves were freed, or bought their freedom, when they got older. [■D] They became Roman citizens and were known as *liberti*, which means men or women who are freed.

* slave: a person who is owned by another person

1 The word them in the passage refers to

Ⓐ people   Ⓑ Roman citizens   Ⓒ slaves   Ⓓ jobs

2 According to paragraph 1, which of the following is true of Ancient Roman society?

Ⓐ Rich people could buy slaves.
Ⓑ A large number of slaves belonged to soldiers.
Ⓒ The wealthy people played an important role in the economy.
Ⓓ The slaves got paid for their work.

3 The word harsh in the passage is closest in meaning to

Ⓐ excellent
Ⓑ dirty
Ⓒ tough
Ⓓ uncomfortable

4 Why does the author mention that these slaves often died after just a few years?

Ⓐ To exaggerate the difficulties that most slaves experienced
Ⓑ To emphasize how badly some slaves were treated
Ⓒ To show that slaves were weak
Ⓓ To describe the work that slaves did

5 According to paragraph 3, all of the following are mentioned as a role of house servants EXCEPT

Ⓐ cooks
Ⓑ nurses
Ⓒ tutors
Ⓓ dressmakers

6 According to paragraph 3, which of the following is NOT true of house servants in Roman times?

Ⓐ They were able to become Roman citizens.
Ⓑ They were skilled in making pottery.
Ⓒ They sometimes taught their owner's children.
Ⓓ They lived in relatively better conditions compared to other slaves.

7 According to the passage, slaves worked in all of the following places EXCEPT

Ⓐ farms
Ⓑ houses
Ⓒ factories
Ⓓ schools

8 Look at the four squares [■] that indicate where the following sentence could be added to the passage.

In fact, house servants in Roman times could have families.

Where would the sentence best fit?

Facts about Roman Slaves

- A rich man might have owned as many as 400 slaves.
- The number of slaves in Rome was about 25% of the total population.
- Slaves were commonly naked when displayed for sale.
- A slave could not legally own property.

The Paleolithic Age

The Paleolithic Age is a prehistoric period that stretches back 2.5 million years. It is noted for the creation of the first stone tools. The climate during the Paleolithic changed and the temperature became warmer. This change in climate affected all life on Earth. In some regions, it enabled humans to produce their own food. Thus, the two things that defined the Paleolithic period were hunting and farming.

Hunting was made possible by adapting tools made of wood, and stone into weapons. These allowed humans to hunt larger animals. Hunting meant that early humans had to be nomadic in order to follow their food sources. As a result, people moved in small bands and did not live in permanent homes. For a long time, Paleolithic people ate fruits, berries and any animals they could catch. Eventually, however, they learned how to farm these things. This provided them with a steady supply of food.

The development of agriculture led to a major change in the way early humans lived. About ten thousand years ago, humans discovered techniques for raising animals and growing certain plants. As people no longer needed to hunt, they had enough time to build permanent homes. Along with this lifestyle came primitive art forms, including pottery and carving. Religious rituals, like burying the dead, also began to occur. While many things took place during the Paleolithic Age, the most important to humankind were changes in climate and technology. Together, these changes allowed humans to evolve from their nomadic lifestyle to a farming-based lifestyle.

* nomadic: moving from place to place
* permanent: long-lasting

1 The word creation in the passage is closest in meaning to

Ⓐ spread   Ⓑ collection   Ⓒ increase   Ⓓ invention

2 According to paragraph 1, what can be inferred about the Paleolithic Age?

Ⓐ Farming could begin with the use of stone tools.
Ⓑ Farming stopped after people began to hunt.
Ⓒ Climate change affected the way prehistoric people live.
Ⓓ Warmer weather made people begin to hunt.

3 The word steady in the passage is closest in meaning to

Ⓐ gradual   Ⓑ permanent   Ⓒ small   Ⓓ constant

4 In paragraph 2, which of the following is NOT mentioned about early humans?

Ⓐ They developed larger tools to hunt larger animals.
Ⓑ They moved from place to place to find food before they actually built homes.
Ⓒ They raised animals to eat.
Ⓓ They ate fruits, berries, and animals.

5 Which of the following best expresses the essential information in the highlighted sentence in the passage? Incorrect answer choices change the meaning in important ways or leave out essential information.

The development of agriculture led to a major change in the way early humans lived.

Ⓐ Early humans made big changes in farming.
Ⓑ People played an important role in changing the way of farming.
Ⓒ Farming allowed early humans to live longer lives.
Ⓓ The lifestyle of early humans changed due to the development of farming.

6 In paragraph 3, the author mentions pottery and carving in order to

Ⓐ show that early humans were too busy to build their homes
Ⓑ provide examples of primitive art forms
Ⓒ show what early humans did to survive
Ⓓ provide areas that early humans are good at

7 According to paragraph 3, a farming-based lifestyle necessarily involves

Ⓐ staying in one place
Ⓑ producing art forms
Ⓒ building large farms
Ⓓ using stone tools

 **Tools from the Paleolithic Age**

- **Hammer Stones**
  Hammer stones were usually made from large, heavy stones. They were held in hand and used for hammering purposes.

- **Hand axes (Choppers)**
  Hand axes were for chopping small wood branches or brush which people used for building materials or firewood.

Reading Helper

A. who

> **Examples from the passage**
> - At first, only the young men **who** wanted to join the church were able to learn.
> (Universities, Line 2)
> - Anyone **who** had enough money could buy them. (Roman Slaves, Line 3)
> - The government owned many men **who** rowed ships as slaves. (Roman Slaves, Line 10)
> - There were a lot of slaves, however, **who** were skilled and worked in factories or craft shops. (Roman Slaves, Line 14)

Complete the sentences using *who* and the phrases from the box.

- is trained to travel in a spacecraft
- can give you advice
- can solve the problem
- want to succeed in the workplace

1 An astronaut is a person _____.

2 The people _____ should like challenges.

3 True friends are the ones _____.

4 Anyone _____ will win the prize.

B. either... or...

> **Examples from the passage**
>
> - In Ancient Rome, a large number of men and women served as slaves of **either** the Roman government **or** wealthy people. (Roman Slaves, Line 1)

Correct the mistakes in the sentences.

1 Sound is interpreted as either music and noise depending on the listener.

→

2 On the Internet, one can find many useful materials either for teaching or for learn.

→

3 Technology can be both good or bad depending on how it's used.

→

UNIT 06
Biology

•• Search! Search!

Find out about the topics using the Internet.
Butterfly Biodiversity, The Evolution of Birds, Cell Theory, Ants and Pheromones

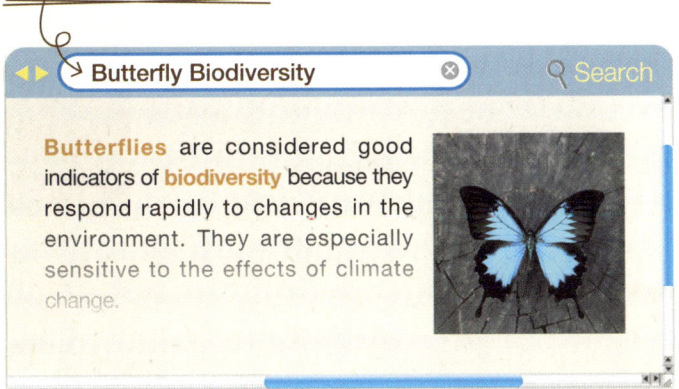

•• Target iBT TOEFL Questions

Insert Text Questions

Look at the four squares [■] that indicate where the following sentence could be added to the passage.

A sentence
Where would the sentence best fit?

Practice 1

Warm Up

1 Look at the picture. What kind of animal is this, a bird or a dinosaur?

2 What are the differences between birds and this animal?

Read the Passage

Your time (1st):   min, (2nd):   min

The Evolution of Birds

The first birds lived around 150 million years ago. Fossils found in Germany are said to be skeletons of prehistoric birds. They were named the <u>Archaeopteryx</u>. Experts believe that these birds represent a <u>genetic</u> link between the birds of today and small two-legged dinosaurs. [■A] The *Archaeopteryx* was first described as a dinosaur. [■B] This was because one of the first fossils found did not reveal feathers. [■C] It allowed people to understand the evolution of birds. [■D]

There are a number of physical similarities between these first birds and birds we see today. Early birds had feathers, wings, and small fingers that seem similar to those of modern birds. There is still debate about whether the feathers of prehistoric birds were used for controlling body temperature or for flying. Unlike birds of today, the first birds had full sets of teeth, flat breastbones, long tails, and three claws on each wing.

Modern birds are highly organized animals. Today, there are more than 10,000 bird species. [■E] The smallest known bird is the bee hummingbird, and the largest is the ostrich. [■F] Modern birds have complex behavior patterns. [■G] These include common habits like nesting, singing, and migrating. Furthermore, most birds alive today have strong legs. [■H] Certain birds, such as ducks and geese, can move around easily in water, on land, and in the air.

* ***Archaeopteryx***: the oldest known bird
* **genetic**: relating to genes

Target iBT TOEFL Questions

1 Look at the four squares [■A]~[■D] that indicate where the following sentence could be added to the passage.

Nevertheless, the link between species that these fossils later revealed was important.

Where would the sentence best fit?

2 Look at the four squares [■E]~[■H] that indicate where the following sentence could be added to the passage.

These allow them to swim, run or walk, and fly.

Where would the sentence best fit?

iBT TOEFL Vocabulary

Fill in the blanks with the appropriate words.

#		
1		**adj** existing in times before recorded history
2		**n** the process through which something develops or changes
3		**n** a discussion, an argument
4		**adv** very, greatly
5		**v** to move seasonally from one area to another

- debate
- evolution
- migrate
- highly
- prehistoric

Biology •• 93

Wrap Up

A Complete the sentences with the appropriate words.

- prehistoric
- evolution
- debate
- highly
- migrate

1. Many animals _____ to areas where there is more food and water.

2. It is _____ dangerous for young children to ride a bike without a helmet.

3. The _____ about global warming is not over.

4. Various tools of today were used in the _____ age.

5. The _____ of birds has been a major topic of discussion in biology.

B Read the passage <The Evolution of Birds> again and categorize the characteristics in the correct category.

Early Birds	Modern Birds

(A) have complex behavior patterns such as nesting, singing, and migrating
(B) have claws on the wings
(C) have a flat breastbone
(D) have strong legs
(E) have teeth

Practice 2

Warm Up

1 According to the following sentence, what can be inferred about the role of cells?

A cell is like a tiny factory.

Read the Passage

Your time (1st): _____ min, (2nd): _____ min

Cell Theory

The cell is the smallest form of life. [■A] As such, the cell is considered to be the key to all life. [■B] In 1665, Robert Hooke created a microscope that allowed him to see "cells" on pieces of wood. [■C] In 1775, a microscope that was ten times more powerful than Hooke's enabled the discovery of single-celled organisms in water. [■D]

However, it was not until the late 19th century that people knew that every living thing had cells. With this knowledge, scientists soon developed a cell theory. [■E] According to the first part of the theory, cells are the building blocks of life. [■F] While some organisms have only one cell, others have many trillions. [■G] Furthermore, different parts of living organisms are made up of different kinds of cells with different functions. [■H]

The second part of cell theory states that all life processes take place within cells. Energy is released in cells. Healing, growth, and reproduction take place in cells. In other words, cells are vital to all life functions.

According to the third part of the theory, new cells are produced from existing cells. At first, living things begin life as a single cell. Later, this cell divides into two cells. Each new cell also divides into two cells. Thus, all life forms today have descended in an unbroken chain from the first basic cells on Earth.

* trillion: a very large indefinite number

Biology ●● 95

Target iBT TOEFL Questions

1 Look at the four squares [■A]~[■D] that indicate where the following sentence could be added to the passage.

Up until the 17th century, however, people knew nothing about cells.

Where would the sentence best fit?

2 Look at the four squares [■E]~[■H] that indicate where the following sentence could be added to the passage.

A human, for example, has hundreds of different kinds of cells.

Where would the sentence best fit?

iBT TOEFL Vocabulary

Fill in the blanks with the appropriate words.

1 _____ n a living thing
2 _____ n what something is used for
3 _____ v to let go of
4 _____ adj critical, basic, key
5 _____ v to separate into parts
6 _____ v to come from

- organism
- function
- vital
- release
- descend
- divide

Wrap Up

A Complete the sentences with the appropriate words.

- organisms
- release
- divided
- vital
- function
- descended

1. The water cycle plays a _____ role in determining the Earth's climate.

2. There are no living _____ on Mars.

3. The _____ of skin is to keep moisture within the body.

4. Stressed plants _____ certain kinds of chemicals.

5. Cells can be _____ into different types.

6. The languages _____ from the Eastern dialect.

B Check (✔) whether the sentences are true (T) or false (F) according to the passage <Cell Theory>.

1. The cell is the smallest form of life. T☐ F☐

2. In 1775, Robert Hooke's microscope discovered single-celled organisms in water. T☐ F☐

3. Living organisms are made up of different kinds of cells. T☐ F☐

4. Not all living things have cells. T☐ F☐

5. Existing cells produce new cells. T☐ F☐

Test 1

Ants and Pheromones

A pheromone is a chemical that triggers a response in another member of the same species. Many living things have the ability to produce pheromones. Flowering plants and mushrooms are also known to use them. Some land animals release this in urine to mark their territory. Probably the most well-known for their use of pheromones, however, are ants. Ants use pheromones to organize their colonies. They are able to detect the taste or smell of a pheromone left by another ant. They do this by moving their antennae.

Ants produce many different pheromones, each with a specific purpose. [■A] For example, they use alarm pheromones to signal danger. [■B] These pheromones may be released in order to warn other ants of danger. [■C] They can be useful when there is a human approaching. [■D] In this case, the release of alarm pheromones will alert all of the other ants about the need to escape. To give directions, they leave pheromone trails that can be followed by other ants. Other kinds of pheromones are used to send away unwanted ants from foreign colonies. Still other pheromones are used to signal that ants must gather at a particular location. Ants also use pheromones to attract members of the opposite sex. These pheromones are useful in mating rituals. Taken together, these different pheromones are vital to the survival of complex ant communities.

* colony: a group of organisms of the same type
* alert: to alarm, to inform
* escape: to run away

1 The word their in the passage refers to

Ⓐ living things
Ⓑ flowering plants and mushrooms
Ⓒ land animals
Ⓓ ants

2 The word detect in the passage is closest in meaning to

Ⓐ sense
Ⓑ use
Ⓒ signal
Ⓓ hear

3 According to paragraph 1, what can be inferred about pheromones?

Ⓐ They send messages to other members of same species.
Ⓑ They are widespread among land animals.
Ⓒ They have a strong smell.
Ⓓ They can only be used by male animals.

4 Look at the four squares [■] that indicate where the following sentence could be added to the passage.

At other times, they may warn of predators like spiders.

Where would the sentence best fit?

5 Why does the author mention a human in paragraph 2?

Ⓐ To show how pheromones can be harmful to humans
Ⓑ To give an example of the use of mating pheromones
Ⓒ To provide a specific case when alarm pheromones can be used
Ⓓ To explain how people can harm ants

6 The word particular in the passage is closest in meaning to

Ⓐ safe
Ⓑ specific
Ⓒ eventual
Ⓓ new

Biology •• 99

7 According to paragraph 2, which of the following is NOT mentioned as a purpose of pheromones?

Ⓐ To inform about danger
Ⓑ To give directions
Ⓒ To attract mates
Ⓓ To kill unwanted ants

8 Which of the following best expresses the essential information in the highlighted sentence? Incorrect answer choices change the meaning in important ways or leave out essential information.

==Taken together, these different pheromones are vital to the survival of complex ant communities.==

Ⓐ In short, ant communities need some pheromones for their survival.
Ⓑ Moreover, pheromones are essential for ants to survive in communities.
Ⓒ In other words, pheromones are necessary for ants to live in different communities.
Ⓓ To summarize, ants need many kinds of pheromones for their survival as a group.

# Different Types of Pheromones

- **Trail pheromones** enable the organisms to return to their nest with food, and also serve as a guide for other members of the same species.
- **Alarm pheromones** are SOS signals to other members of the same species. They also warn other members of danger.
- **Territorial pheromones** define the territory of the species.
- **Mating pheromones** are used to attract members of the opposite sex.

Butterfly Biodiversity

Butterflies are beautiful insects that are popular with the public. They also play an important role in the reproduction of flowers. Furthermore, they are necessary food sources for birds. They are also useful for scientific study, especially the study of biodiversity. Biodiversity is the number and variety of plants, animals, and insects in an environment.

Butterflies are considered good indicators of biodiversity because they respond rapidly to changes in the environment. They are especially sensitive to the effects of climate change. Simply speaking, a healthy environment means it has a large number of butterflies.

As a representative of many other insects, butterflies are well documented. In 1875, a biologist in the Amazon noted that there were about 700 species of butterflies. Meanwhile, the British Isles were home to no more than 66 species and continental Europe had only 321 species. Through such research, ninety percent of the world's butterfly species have been given scientific names.

Butterflies are caught using a net. They are then transferred into a jar and killed using chemicals. [■A] The butterflies are then photographed. [■B] Given the hundreds of butterflies that need to be identified, this process is both difficult and time consuming. [■C] As a result, mistakes often happen. [■D] However, scientists hope to limit the number of mistakes in the process of sorting butterfly species. It is important that they succeed because butterflies are very useful for studying environmental changes.

* **representative:** a typical example of something
* **time consuming:** requiring a lot of time
* **sort:** to categorize, to divide into categories

1 According to paragraph 1, which of the following is NOT mentioned as a role of butterflies?

Ⓐ They indicate the location of birds.
Ⓑ They help flowers reproduce.
Ⓒ They are used in scientific studies.
Ⓓ They are food sources for birds.

2 According to paragraph 2, butterflies are considered to be a good indicator of biodiversity because

Ⓐ they change their behavior according to the climate
Ⓑ they can only live in a clean environment
Ⓒ they reflect insect populations
Ⓓ they respond quickly to changes in the environment

3 According to paragraphs 2 and 3, what can be inferred about Amazon?

Ⓐ Amazon does not have a stable climate.
Ⓑ Amazon is wider than British Isles.
Ⓒ Amazon has a relatively healthy environment.
Ⓓ There are ninety percent of all butterflies.

4 Which of the following best expresses the essential information in the highlighted sentence in the passage? Incorrect answer choices change the meaning in important ways or leave out essential information.

> Through such research, ninety percent of the world's butterfly species have been given scientific names.

Ⓐ All species of butterflies in the world have their own names.
Ⓑ Researchers have named ninety percent of all butterflies.
Ⓒ Research has allowed ninety percent of butterfly species to have scientific names.
Ⓓ Scientific names are given to some of the butterfly species through a lot of research.

5 The word <mark>transferred</mark> in the passage is closest in meaning to

Ⓐ divided
Ⓑ moved
Ⓒ placed
Ⓓ packed

6 Look at the four squares [■] that indicate where the following sentence could be added to the passage.

These pictures are used to identify different species.

Where would the sentence best fit?

7 The word <mark>they</mark> in the passage refers to

Ⓐ scientists
Ⓑ mistakes
Ⓒ butterflies
Ⓓ impacts

| More to know | **Facts about Butterflies** |

- Butterflies represent a vast food source for predators.
- Butterflies are significant plant pollinators. If plants are not pollinated, seeds and fruits are not produced.
- The presence of butterflies indicates the overall well-being of the ecosystem.
- Unlike other insects, butterflies neither bite, sting, nor transmit disease.

Reading Helper

A. whether... or

> **Examples from the passage**
> - There is still debate about **whether** the feathers of prehistoric birds were used for controlling body temperature **or** for flying.   (The Evolution of Birds, Line 9)

Make sentences using the words given in the parentheses.

1 It wasn't clear (over the phone / the survey / whether / was performed in person / or).

→

2 The new online service shows (a book / or / is in the library / whether / checked out by someone).

→

B. unlike

> **Examples from the passage**
> - **Unlike** birds of today, the first birds had full sets of teeth, flat breastbones, long tails, and three claws on each wing.   (The Evolution of Birds, Line 10)

Which of the following sentences are closest in meaning to the initial sentence?

1 Unlike bees, wasps can sting more than once.

  (A) Bees are able to sting several times.

  (B) Bees can sting only once.

2 Unlike their parents, today's children are growing up with computers.

    (A) Computers were not available for parents when they were growing up.

    (B) Unlike their parents, today's children cannot live without computers.

C. it was not until ~ that

> **Examples from the passage**
>
> • However, **it was not until** the late 19th century that people knew **that** every living thing had cells. (Cell Theory, Line 7)

Rewrite the following sentences using the expression *it was not until ~ that*.

1 It became possible to produce books quickly. (the 15th century)

→

2 The PhD was offered for the first time. (the 20th century)

→

UNIT 07
Sociology

•• Search! Search!

Find out about the topics using the Internet.
The Industrial Revolution, Types of Leaders, Types of Society, Surveys

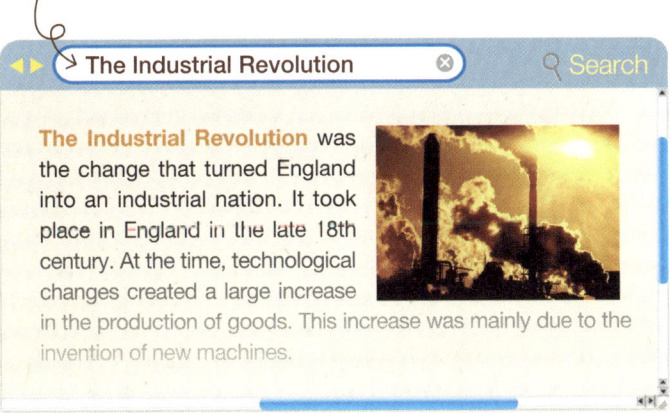

•• Target iBT TOEFL Questions

Categorization Questions

Directions: Complete the table below about the two types of _____ discussed in the passage. Match the appropriate phrases/statements to the types of _____ with which they are associated. Two of the answer choices will NOT be used.

Answer Choices

Ⓐ ~ Ⓖ

Category 1
- _____
- _____
- _____

Category 2
- _____
- _____

Practice 1

Warm Up

1 Who were history's great leaders in your country?

2 What makes a good leader? List several qualities.

○ _____   ○ _____   ○ _____

Read the Passage

Your time (1st):   min, (2nd):   min

Types of Leaders

In families, it is common for the parents to be the leaders. In groups of friends, it is also common for one to be the leader. While many people think that leaders are born with special skills, research has shown that there is no such thing as a "natural leader". Moreover, research shows that there are often groups with more than one leader. In fact, most groups have two different kinds of leaders. The first is an instrumental leader and the second is an expressive leader.

An instrumental leader focuses on finishing jobs. Group members look to the instrumental leader to get work done. Instrumental leaders are likely to have distant relationships to other group members. They give orders. They also <u>discipline</u> members who slow the group down.

On the other hand, an expressive leader focuses on harmony among members. They are concerned with giving emotional support to other members of the group. They also try to keep peace within a group. Expressive leaders often make friends with the group members. This allows them to offer sympathy when someone faces difficulties. It also enables them to use humor to overcome problems that might divide the group. Because of the nature of their role, expressive leaders develop much closer relationships with their group members than instrumental leaders. In the end, however, a group is most successful when both styles of leadership work together.

* discipline: to provide a rule of behavior

Target iBT TOEFL Questions

1 Directions: Complete the table below about the types of leaders discussed in the passage. Match the appropriate phrases to the types with which they are associated. TWO of the answer choices will NOT be used.

Answer Choices

Ⓐ are natural leaders
Ⓑ provide support to individual members
Ⓒ enjoy a distant respect
Ⓓ have close relationships with group members
Ⓔ slow the members down
Ⓕ focus on goals
Ⓖ give emotional support

Expressive Leaders

- _____
- _____
- _____

Instrumental Leaders

- _____
- _____

iBT TOEFL Vocabulary

Fill in the blanks with the appropriate words.

1. _____ **adj** far apart
2. _____ **n** a command, an instruction given by someone with authority
3. _____ **v** to provide a rule of behavior
4. _____ **n** a feeling of support
5. _____ **v** to provide, to give

- sympathy
- offer
- distant
- order (n)
- discipline (v)

Wrap Up

A Complete the sentences with the appropriate words.

- offer
- orders
- sympathy
- discipline
- distant

1. The two people are _____ relatives. They only see each other at family reunions once a year.

2. Parents should _____ their children by limiting the time they can play computer games.

3. Some schools _____ religious education.

4. The government expressed great _____ for the victims.

5. Leadership is more than simply giving _____ .

B Correct the underlined words to complete the summary note of the passage <Types of Leaders>.

> Paragraph 1: Most social groups have two different kinds of leaders:
> (1) an instrumental leader (2) an expressive leader
>
> Paragraph 2: Instrumental Leaders
> - focus on finishing jobs
> - have <u>close</u> relationships with group members
> - give <u>advice</u> or discipline members
>
> Paragraph 3: Expressive Leaders
> - give <u>financial</u> support
> - keep peace within a group
> - make friends with group <u>leaders</u>

Practice 2

Warm Up

1 Identify the topic and read the passage quickly. What do you think the passage is about?

☐ Before and after the Industrial Revolution

☐ The causes of the Industrial Revolution

Read the Passage

Your time (1ˢᵗ): ____ min, (2ⁿᵈ): ____ min

The Industrial Revolution

The Industrial Revolution was the change that turned England into an industrial nation. It took place in England in the late 18th century. At the time, technological changes created a large increase in the production of goods. This increase was mainly due to the invention of new machines.

Before the Industrial Revolution, products were either made by hand or by using simple machines. Most people worked at home in rural areas. Only a small number of people made things in workshops in towns. At this time, it was hard to keep in touch with other people. News was spread by travelers or through messengers. Goods were mostly sold within the area in which they were produced. Additionally, the quality of education was poor.

However, after the revolution, things were much different. Factories brought workers together. Power-driven machines like the steam engine replaced handwork. These machines made production faster and easier than ever before. By the end of the 19th century, life also changed in many ways. The government created new laws regulating work in factories. Even so, people worked close to 70 hours per week. Moreover, children in most families had to work as well. Meanwhile, banks became a very important part of this new economy. This was because they controlled the money that was used to purchase and operate the factories.

Target iBT TOEFL Questions

1 Directions: Complete the table below about the Industrial Revolution discussed in the passage. Match the appropriate statements to the periods with which they are asssociated. TWO of the answer choices will NOT be used.

Answer Choices

Ⓐ New laws were made to control work in factories.
Ⓑ Banks appeared for the first time.
Ⓒ Some children worked in factories.
Ⓓ Children had to work almost 70 hours per week.
Ⓔ Many of the products were made by hand.
Ⓕ Products were sold locally.
Ⓖ Steam engines began to be used.

After the Revolution
-
-
-

Before the Revolution
-
-

iBT TOEFL Vocabulary

Fill in the blanks with the appropriate words.

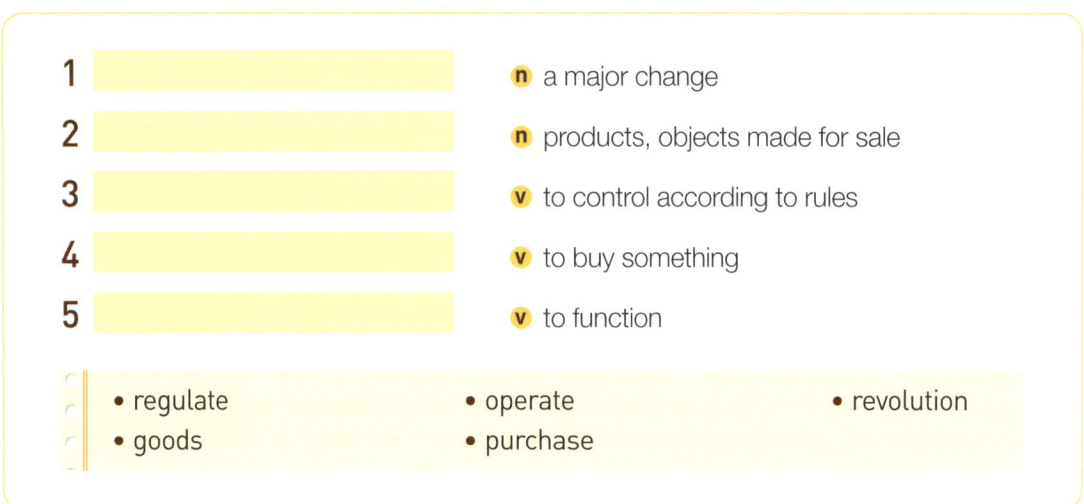

1. _____ ⓝ a major change
2. _____ ⓝ products, objects made for sale
3. _____ ⓥ to control according to rules
4. _____ ⓥ to buy something
5. _____ ⓥ to function

- regulate
- operate
- revolution
- goods
- purchase

Wrap Up

A Complete the sentences with the appropriate words.

- goods
- operated
- regulate
- revolution
- purchase

1 The system should be _____ 24 hours a day.

2 The _____ were delivered directly to the customers.

3 Female consumers tend to _____ items online.

4 The technological _____ will change our way of life.

5 The government should _____ violence on TV.

B Fill in the blanks with the information provided in the passage <The Industrial Revolution>.

- Before the Industrial Revolution, products were either made by _____ or by using simple machines.
  → After the Revolution, products began to be produced in _____.

- Before the Industrial Revolution, many people in _____ areas worked at home.
  → Many people worked in factories by the end of the 19th century. Even some _____ had to work as well.

Types of Society

[■A] Pre-state societies were organized around villages. [■B] State-organized societies evolved out of these pre-state societies over thousands of years. [■C] This change came with the emergence of food production. [■D] To better understand the differences between the two societies, it is necessary to look closely at both types.

Pre-state societies were small-sized societies. They were based on the village. They were different in terms of political systems. While some village-based societies had no central authority, others were operated under the authority of a hereditary leader. However, all pre-state societies lacked a highly organized class structure. They also lacked other characteristics of state-organized societies.

In contrast, state-organized societies operate on a large scale. They also share a number of common features. First, all states are run by a centralized political structure. Second, there is a strict social order. The elite hold all power. Most people of the state are common people such as farmers and other food producers. Slaves are at the bottom of the social order. Because of this, social inequality is a reality for many states. Another common feature of states is intense food production. It is often supported by water control systems such as irrigation. Public buildings are also a distinctive characteristic of states. Many of them serve as temples or housing for the elite. Ancient Rome was a great example of a highly complex state-organized society.

* hereditary: passed from a parent to their child
* distinctive: special, unique

1 Look at the four squares [■] that indicate where the following sentence could be added to the passage.

Different kinds of societies can be explained based on the way they are organized.

Where would the sentence best fit?

2 The word emergence in the passage is closest in meaning to

Ⓐ limitation
Ⓑ introduction
Ⓒ increase
Ⓓ crisis

3 Which of the following best expresses the essential information in the highlighted sentence in the passage? Incorrect answer choices change the meaning in important ways or leave out essential information.

To better understand the differences between the two societies, it is necessary to look closely at both types.

Ⓐ We can understand the two societies better by looking at them closely.
Ⓑ To understand the societies, the similarities between them need to be studied.
Ⓒ It is necessary to understand the differences between the two societies.
Ⓓ The differences will be better understood if we look at the two societies closely.

4 The word common in the passage is closest in meaning to

Ⓐ typical
Ⓑ popular
Ⓒ strong
Ⓓ random

5 The word It in the passage refers to

Ⓐ centralized political structure
Ⓑ state
Ⓒ food production
Ⓓ irrigation

6 According to paragraph 3, many states were not equal because

　Ⓐ they had a centralized political structure
　Ⓑ the common people had slaves
　Ⓒ the elite had no authority
　Ⓓ they had hierarchical social classes

7 **Directions:** Complete the table below about the types of societies discussed in the passage. Match the appropriate phrases to the types with which they are associated. TWO of the answer choices will NOT be used.

Answer Choices

Ⓐ were based on villages
Ⓑ produced food
Ⓒ were not run by an authority
Ⓓ lacked a highly organized class structure
Ⓔ were operated by a political structure
Ⓕ had different social classes
Ⓖ were from pre-state societies

State-organized Societies
- _____
- _____
- _____

Pre-state Societies
- _____
- _____

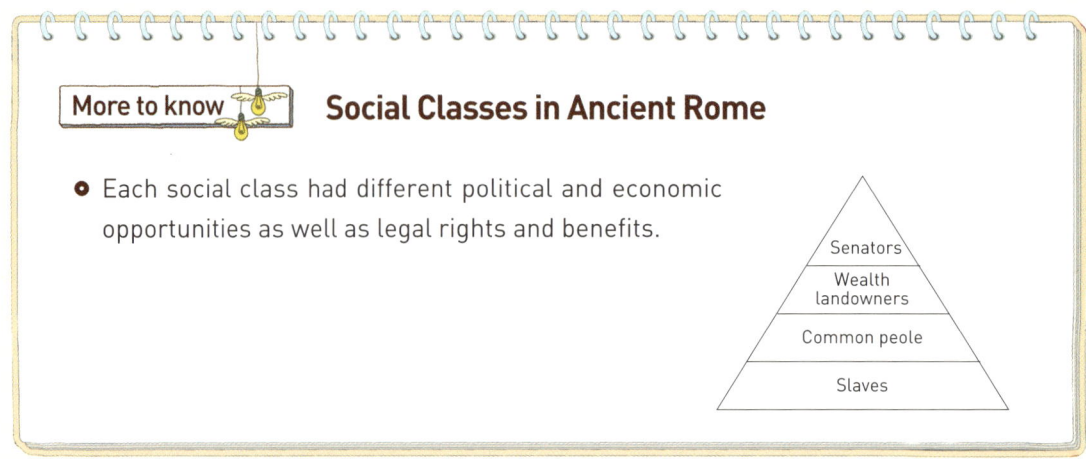

| More to know | **Social Classes in Ancient Rome** |

- Each social class had different political and economic opportunities as well as legal rights and benefits.

Test 2

TOEFL Reading

PAUSE TEST | SECTION EXIT

REVIEW | HELP | OK | NEXT

Surveys

A survey is a study that is used to gather information. [■A] Many different methods are used for gathering information. The size of a survey is one way. The other way is to focus on a certain group of people. [■B] This process is commonly based on categories such as age, gender, and occupation. [■C] In addition, surveys can be conducted from local to national areas. [■D]

Oral interviews are probably the most well-known method. As they are often done face-to-face, oral interviews are also the most direct method. However, they are not very accurate in representing the total population. Oral interviews tend to be biased towards people who always go to the interview location. It is also true that this type of interview attracts people who want attention, while it drives away people who are shy.

[■E] Questionnaires are another popular kind of survey. [■F] Questionnaires have access to every level of society because they are usually sent by mail. [■G] Mailed questionnaires are good at avoiding visible biases like age, gender, and nationality. Moreover, interviewees tend to be more honest in answering questions privately in their own homes. [■H] Because questionnaires are indirect, however, they are often thrown away. Thus, the cost of mailing questionnaires seldom produces equal results. In the end, results from surveys can be seen all around us. Regardless of the way it is gathered, information from surveys influences news coverage and advertising.

* biased: favoring one side to another

UNIT 7

1 Look at the four squares [■A] ~ [■D] that indicate where the following sentence could be added to the passage.

Among the many kinds of surveys used, the two most popular are oral interviews and questionnaires.

Where would the sentence best fit?

2 The word conducted in the passage is closest in meaning to

Ⓐ printed　　　Ⓑ created　　　Ⓒ performed　　　Ⓓ considered

3 The word accurate in the passage is closest in meaning to

Ⓐ correct　　　Ⓑ large　　　Ⓒ good　　　Ⓓ popular

4 Which of the following best expresses the essential information in the highlighted sentence in the passage? Incorrect answer choices change the meaning in important ways or leave out essential information.

It is also true that this type of interview attracts people who want attention, while it drives away people who are shy.

Ⓐ While attractive people enjoy this type of interview, shy people avoid it.
Ⓑ Shy people avoid oral interviews, unlike people who look for attention.
Ⓒ Oral interviews provide an opportunity for people who want attention.
Ⓓ Attention seekers drive away shy people when they participate in oral interviews.

5 According to paragraph 2, oral interviews are the most direct method because

Ⓐ they access every level of society
Ⓑ they are popular among people
Ⓒ people participate voluntarily
Ⓓ the information is gathered in person

6 Look at the four squares [■E] ~ [■H] that indicate where the following sentence could be added to the passage.

This means that the interviewees are chosen more randomly.

Where would the sentence best fit?

7 The word seldom in the passage is closest in meaning to

Ⓐ mostly　　　Ⓑ roughly　　　Ⓒ truly　　　Ⓓ hardly

8 The word it in the passage refers to

Ⓐ cost   Ⓑ way   Ⓒ information   Ⓓ news coverage

9 Directions: Complete the table below about the types of surveys discussed in the passage. Match the appropriate phrases to the types with which they are associated. TWO of the answer choices will NOT be used.

Answer Choices

Ⓐ require personal contact
Ⓑ can reach every level of society
Ⓒ tend to exclude shy people
Ⓓ cost a lot
Ⓔ often show low response rates
Ⓕ usually gather information by e-mails
Ⓖ are not influenced by the first impression of the people

Questionnaires

• _____
• _____
• _____

Oral Interviews

• _____
• _____

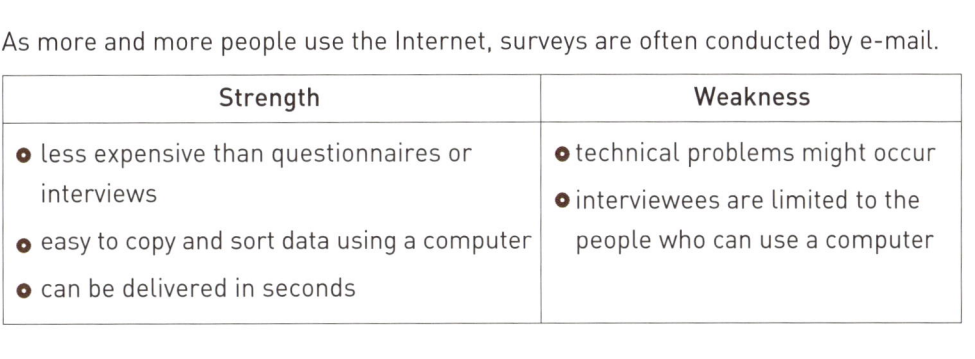

| More to know | **E-mail Surveys** |

As more and more people use the Internet, surveys are often conducted by e-mail.

Strength	Weakness
• less expensive than questionnaires or interviews • easy to copy and sort data using a computer • can be delivered in seconds	• technical problems might occur • interviewees are limited to the people who can use a computer

Sociology •• 119

Reading Helper

A. while (but, whereas)

> **Examples from the passage**
> - It is also true that this type of interview attracts people who want attention, **while** it drives away people who are shy. (Surveys, Line 10)
> - **While** some village-based societies had no central authority, others were operated under the authority of a hereditary leader. (Types of Society, Line 7)
> - **While** many people think that leaders are born with special skills, research has shown that there is no such thing as a "natural leader". (Types of Leaders, Line 2)

Combine the two sentences using *while*.

1 Some people support the environment. Others destroy the environment.

→

2 Air pollution increases. Quality of life decreases.

→

B. allow ... to do

> **Examples from the passage**
> - This **allows** them **to** offer sympathy when someone faces difficulties. (Types of Leaders, Line 14)

C. enable ... to do

> **Examples from the passage**
> • It also **enables** them **to** use humor to overcome problems that might divide the group.
> (Types of Leaders, Line 15)

Correct the mistakes in the sentences.

1 The information allowed people understanding complicated facts more easily.

→

2 The project enabled the students trying various strategies.

→

3 The website will enable consumers compare the prices of the products.

→

4 Mild weather allowed to stay the birds in this area.

→

UNIT 08
Geology

•• Search! Search!

Find out about the topics using the Internet.
Deserts, Ecosystems, Volcanoes, Fossils

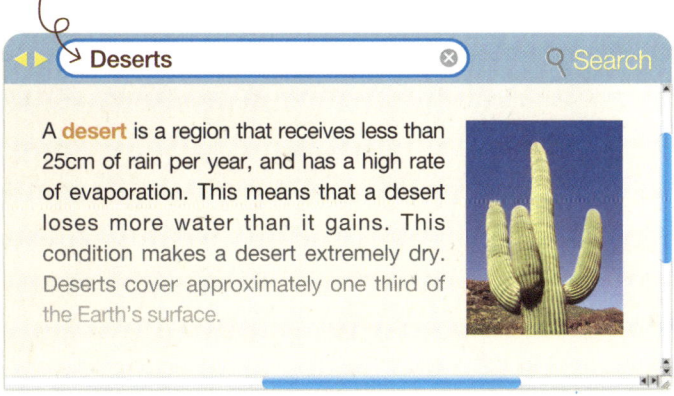

•• Target iBT TOEFL Questions

Summary Questions

Directions: An introductory sentence for a brief summary of the passage is provided below. Complete the summary by selecting the THREE answer choices that express important ideas in the passage. Some sentences do not belong in the summary because they express ideas that are not presented in the passage or are minor ideas in the passage.

An introductory sentence

-
-
-

Answer Choices

Ⓐ ~ Ⓕ

Practice 1

Warm Up

1. Go through the passage quickly to find these words. Guess what the topic is about using the words.

- ecosystem
- connected
- producers
- consumers
- decomposers

Read the Passage

Ecosystems

Everything in the natural world is connected. An ecosystem is a community of living and non-living things that work together. Living things include plants and animals. Non-living things include water, light, and soil. Ecosystems can be as large as an ocean, or as small as a drop of water. To create a balanced system, all of the components of an ecosystem must work together.

The living organisms in an ecosystem can be divided into three categories: producers, consumers, and decomposers. Producers are green plants which make their own food from sunlight, nutrients, and water. Consumers are animals. They get their energy from producers or from organisms that eat producers. Consumers are organized into three categories: herbivores, carnivores, and omnivores. Herbivores feed only on plants. Carnivores feed on herbivores and other carnivores. Omnivores eat both plants and other animals. Finally, decomposers are plants and animals that break down dead organisms into nutrients. Decomposers complete the system, returning nutrients to the soil.

Essentially, the living and non-living things in an ecosystem depend upon one another to survive. A healthy ecosystem has a lot of variety. Therefore, it is less likely to be damaged by human interaction, natural disasters, and changes in climate. Each species in an ecosystem has a specific role which keeps the system healthy. By studying and maintaining diversity, we help keep our planet healthy.

Target iBT TOEFL Questions

1 Directions: An introductory sentence for a brief summary of the passage is provided below. Complete the summary by selecting the THREE answer choices that express important ideas in the passage. Some sentences do not belong in the summary because they express ideas that are not presented in the passage or are minor ideas in the passage.

An ecosystem is the basic unit of nature.

-
-
-

Answer Choices

Ⓐ An ecosystem consists of living and non-living organisms.
Ⓑ The living and non-living organisms interact with each other in an ecosystem.
Ⓒ Consumers can be divided into three categories.
Ⓓ Decomposers make the system healthy.
Ⓔ Living organisms can be categorized as producers, consumers, and decomposers, and they play specific roles in an ecosystem.
Ⓕ An ecosystem consists of three levels: herbivores, carnivores, and omnivores.

iBT TOEFL Vocabulary

Fill in the blanks with the appropriate words.

1 _____	**n**	a part of something
2 _____	**v**	to keep in a certain state
3 _____	**adv**	basically
4 _____	**n**	an animal that usually feeds on other animals
5 _____	**n**	an animal that feeds on plants
6 _____	**n**	an animal that feeds on both plants and other animals

- essentially
- maintain
- component
- herbivore
- omnivore
- carnivore

Geology •• 125

Wrap Up

A Complete the sentences with the appropriate words.

> • component • carnivores • herbivores
> • essentially • maintain • omnivores

1 Asking questions is an important _____ of the learning process.

2 Another term for _____ is 'meat eaters'.

3 _____ do not eat meat. Examples of these animals are rabbits and deer.

4 _____ are animals that consume both animals and plants in their typical diet.

5 While pens and pencils are _____ both writing tools, their main difference is that pencils are erasable.

6 It is important to _____ peace in society.

B Fill in the blanks with the appropriate words based on the information in the passage <Ecosystems>.

• carnivores
• herbivores
• producers
• decomposers
• omnivores

Practice 2

Warm Up

1 Choose some environmental characteristics of desert.

- dry   • sandy   • warm   • humid   • hot   • rainy

2 Name a few desert animals or plants.

Read the Passage

Your time (1st): _____ min, (2nd): _____ min

Deserts

A desert is a region that receives less than 25cm of rain per year and has a high rate of evaporation. This means that a desert loses more water than it gains. This condition makes a desert extremely dry. Deserts cover approximately one third of the Earth's surface.

To survive in the desert, living things must be able to live on very little water. Also, they must be able to adapt to extreme heat. Many animals have adapted to live in deserts. They have found ways to use less water and keep cool. Some are nocturnal creatures. They live underground during the day to avoid the hot sun. Plants have also adapted to these extreme conditions. Some cacti have shallow roots that spread out widely to collect water. Others develop small, spiny leaves that release less moisture. A large range of plants survive in deserts. These plants also help support the life of desert animals.

Rain does occasionally fall in deserts. Water from rainfall higher in the backs of valleys travels down to deserts. This water only lasts a few days, but leaves rich minerals behind. Iron, gold, and silver are some of the minerals found in deserts. Deserts are also potentially huge sources for solar energy because of their vast area exposed to the Sun. Because of this, deserts may prove to be highly valuable resources in the near future.

* nocturnal: active during the night

Target iBT TOEFL Questions

1 Directions: An introductory sentence for a brief summary of the passage is provided below. Complete the summary by selecting the THREE answer choices that express important ideas in the passage. Some sentences do not belong in the summary because they express ideas that are not presented in the passage or are minor ideas in the passage.

The desert is not a wasteland.

-
-
-

Answer Choices

Ⓐ A large number of plants found in deserts have their own ways of preserving water.
Ⓑ Mineral resources include iron, gold, and silver.
Ⓒ Deserts cover one third of the Earth's surface.
Ⓓ In a desert, more water is lost than received.
Ⓔ Many species of animals have adapted to desert environments.
Ⓕ Deserts have many mineral resources.

iBT TOEFL Vocabulary

Fill in the blanks with the appropriate words.

1		**adj** having worth, very important
2		**n** an area, a place
3		**adv** roughly, more or less
4		**adj** wide in range
5		**adv** from time to time
6		**adv** with a possibility of becoming actual, possibly

- approximately
- occasionally
- region
- vast
- valuable
- potentially

Wrap Up

A Find the synonyms for the underlined words.

- approximately
- occasionally
- region
- vast
- valuable
- potentially

1 <u>Roughly</u> 500 people gathered for the ceremony.

2 The northern part of Alaska is <u>an area</u> described as arctic.

3 A <u>large</u> amount of information is available on the Internet.

4 The experience provided <u>important</u> lessons about the role of parents.

5 The group met <u>from time to time</u> to encourage each other.

6 The effect of the decision is <u>possibly</u> huge.

B Check (✔) whether the sentences are True (T) or False (F) according to the passage <Deserts>.

1 Deserts receive less than 15cm of rain per year.   T☐ F☐

2 Deserts cover almost 1/3 of the Earth's surface.   T☐ F☐

3 Only a few animals have successfully adapted to desert life.   T☐ F☐

4 Rainfall leaves behind rich minerals.   T☐ F☐

5 Some cacti have deep roots to collect water.   T☐ F☐

Geology •• 129

Volcanoes

The motivation for predicting when a volcano will erupt is to protect lives. There have been many disasters from volcanic eruptions in the past. In 79 AD, Mount Vesuvius in Italy erupted and buried two cities. Thousands of people were killed.

Since then, scientists have found a way to use knowledge of the volcano's eruptive history. They collect data and interpret it to predict when an eruption will occur. However, this method is not always accurate. It can lead to improper conclusions about a volcano's impact on the surrounding area.

Modern science has also developed ways to consistently forecast future eruptions. Scientists study how volcanoes change before they erupt. There are a few ways that volcanoes change before exploding. Sometimes, the shape of volcanoes changes before they explode. Also, the ground near a volcano becomes more active. Additionally, the gas inside a volcano changes before it erupts. Scientists can use all of these changes to watch volcanoes. If they see changes occurring they may predict an eruption.

Even though scientists can observe the changes of volcanoes, they sometimes fail to predict eruptions. This happened in Africa in 2002. Scientists noticed some changes in the mountain. However, the changes seemed too small to be dangerous to nearby towns. After the volcano erupted, 150,000 people were left homeless. Scientists hope they can make more accurate predictions in the future.

1. Which of the following best expresses the essential information in the highlighted sentence in the passage? Incorrect answer choices change the meaning in important ways or leave out essential information.

   The motivation for predicting when a volcano will erupt is to protect lives.

   Ⓐ The reason scientists predict eruptions is to save people's lives.
   Ⓑ To save people, volcano eruptions need to be predicted.
   Ⓒ The most important thing about predicting volcanoes is the nearby people.
   Ⓓ Lives can be protected if there are no volcano eruptions.

2. The word improper in the passage is closest in meaning to

   Ⓐ wrong   Ⓑ fair   Ⓒ direct   Ⓓ instant

3. The word it in the passage refers to

   Ⓐ ground   Ⓑ shape   Ⓒ gas   Ⓓ volcano

4. According to paragraph 3, all of the following are mentioned as a change before exploding EXCEPT

   Ⓐ the shape of a volcano
   Ⓑ the surrounding ground
   Ⓒ the gas inside a volcano
   Ⓓ the sound inside a volcano

5. According to paragraph 4, scientists failed to predict a volcanic eruption in 2002 because

   Ⓐ they collected the wrong data
   Ⓑ there was not enough information
   Ⓒ they thought the changes they observed were minor
   Ⓓ they did not recognize the changes in the mountain

UNIT 8

Geology •• 131

6 According to paragraph 4, what can be inferred about the predictions of volcanic activity?

Ⓐ Scientists will find a perfect solution for predicting volcanic eruptions.
Ⓑ There should be enough information to make a correct decision.
Ⓒ The scientist who interprets the data has an important role.
Ⓓ Small changes in volcanoes can be ignored in predicting eruptions.

7 **Directions**: An introductory sentence for a brief summary of the passage is provided below. Complete the summary by selecting the THREE answer choices that express important ideas in the passage. Some sentences do not belong in the summary because they express ideas that are not presented in the passage or are minor ideas in the passage.

Scientists play an important role in predicting volcanic eruptions.

-
-
-

Answer Choices

Ⓐ Scientists have found a way to use the history of volcanic eruptions to save people's lives.
Ⓑ How a volcano changes before exploding can be an important element in predicting eruptions.
Ⓒ Scientists hope to find a perfect way to predict eruptions in the future.
Ⓓ People have been trying to predict volcanic eruptions for many years.
Ⓔ Mount Vesuvius erupted and buried two cities.
Ⓕ Scientists have failed to find a perfect way to know when volcanoes will erupt.

| More to know  | **Facts about Volcanoes** |

- More than 80% of the Earth's surface is formed by volcanic eruptions.
- There are more than 1,500 active volcanoes in the world.
- Indonesia has, by far, the most volcanoes.
- The largest volcano on Earth is Mauna Loa in Hawaii.

Fossils

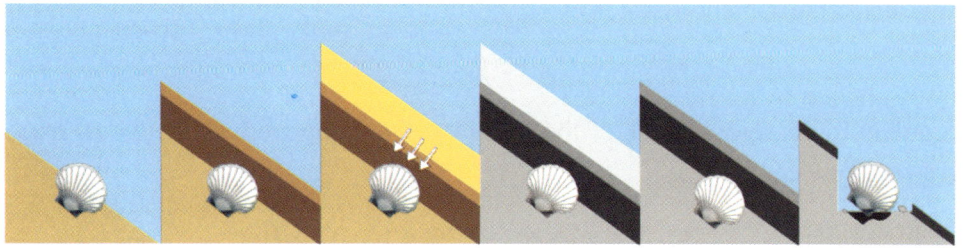

1. Death   2. Deposition   3. Sedimentation   4. Mineralization   5. Erosion   6. Exposure

<The Process of Fossilization>

A fossil is the remains of a creature that existed long ago. Having died, an organism gets covered with sand. The body of the creature then begins to decay. After only a few weeks, all that remains is the hard part of the body, such as bones and shells. After several months, the creature gradually becomes covered with layers of sediment. Eventually, more and more layers are deposited, creating pressure. [■A] Over millions of years, minerals replace the hard parts of the body. Through this process, the hard parts are converted into rock. [■B] The fossil that remains has the same shape as the original object, but the color is different. [■C] Later, as the Earth's plates move, the fossil is finally exposed. [■D] Other factors such as wind, rain, ice, and erosion also help exposure to occur.

Not all previous life forms are preserved as fossils. In fact, the vast majority simply disappeared without a trace. This is because fossilization only occurs under certain circumstances. First, the dead organism must be buried quickly. It is important that it is not exposed to bacteria, weather, or erosion. Thus, swamps have always been a prime location for fossilization. In addition, larger organisms with hard body parts are more likely to become fossilized. Because of this, only a small number of organisms have been preserved as fossils.

* **sediment:** a layer of sand, stone etc.
* **erosion:** condition in which the surface of land is worn away by water or wind

1. The word **converted** in the passage is closest in meaning to
   - Ⓐ buried
   - Ⓑ saved
   - Ⓒ categorized
   - Ⓓ changed

2. Look at the four squares [■] that indicate where the following sentence could be added to the passage.

   These layers also protect the body from damage.

   Where would the sentence best fit?

3. According to paragraph 1, all of the following are mentioned as factors of exposure EXCEPT
   - Ⓐ color changes
   - Ⓑ the movement of the Earth's plates
   - Ⓒ weather changes
   - Ⓓ erosion

4. The word **preserved** in the passage is closest in meaning to
   - Ⓐ treated
   - Ⓑ known
   - Ⓒ maintained
   - Ⓓ classed

5. The word **prime** in the passage is closest in meaning to
   - Ⓐ ideal
   - Ⓑ necessary
   - Ⓒ special
   - Ⓓ bad

6. Which of the following best expresses the essential information in the highlighted sentence in the passage? Incorrect answer choices change the meaning in important ways or leave out essential information.

   Because of this, only a small number of organisms have been preserved as fossils.
   - Ⓐ Only a limited part of living things have been preserved as fossils.
   - Ⓑ Because of these rare conditions, it is hard to find fossils.
   - Ⓒ Due to this fact, fossil preservation rarely occurs.
   - Ⓓ All living organisms could become fossils because of this reason.

7 According to paragraph 2, the vast majority of former organisms disappeared because

  Ⓐ fossilization requires certain circumstances
  Ⓑ they were exposed to bacteria
  Ⓒ they were buried quickly
  Ⓓ they were not buried in a swamp

8 According to paragraph 2, which of the following is NOT mentioned as a good condition for fossilization?

  Ⓐ The organisms need to be buried quickly.
  Ⓑ The organisms should be protected from decay or erosion.
  Ⓒ The organisms should be large and have hard body parts.
  Ⓓ The organisms must live in swamps.

9 **Directions**: An introductory sentence for a brief summary of the passage is provided below. Complete the summary by selecting the THREE answer choices that express important ideas in the passage. Some sentences do not belong in the summary because they express ideas that are not presented in the passage or are minor ideas in the passage.

The process of fossilization rarely occurs.

-
-
-

Answer Choices

  Ⓐ Larger creatures with hard body parts are more likely to be fossilized.
  Ⓑ There are many different fossil types.
  Ⓒ Fossilization occurs as a result of many different processes.
  Ⓓ Fossilization requires certain circumstances, such as rapid burial.
  Ⓔ Only a small number of large animals can be fossilized.
  Ⓕ Some examples of fossils are bones, footprints, and plant leaves.

Reading Helper

A. before / after

> **Examples from the passage**
> - Scientists study how volcanoes change **before** they erupt. (Volcanoes, Line 11)
> - Sometimes, the shape of volcanoes changes **before** they explode. (Volcanoes, Line 12)
> - Additionally, the gas inside a volcano changes **before** it erupts. (Volcanoes, Line 14)
> - **After** the volcano erupted, 150,000 people were left homeless. (Volcanoes, Line 20)

Combine the two sentences into one using either *before* or *after* as it appears in the parentheses.

1 Bears eat a large amount food. They go into hibernation. (before)

→

2 It takes time for astronauts to feel comfortable with standing. They return to Earth. (after)

→

3 People carry the virus in their bodies for many weeks. The disease develops. (before)

→

B. which

> **Examples from the passage**
>
> • Producers are green plants **which** make their own food from sunlight, nutrients, and water.
> (Ecosystems, Line 7)
>
> • Each species in an ecosystem has a specific role **which** keeps the system healthy.
> (Ecosystems, Line 18)

Combine the two sentences into one using *which*.

1 The company developed a new system. It allows users to access information more easily.

→

2 An ant nest has one female ant. It lays eggs.

→

3 The features are grouped into categories. These categories have smaller categories.

→

Actual Test

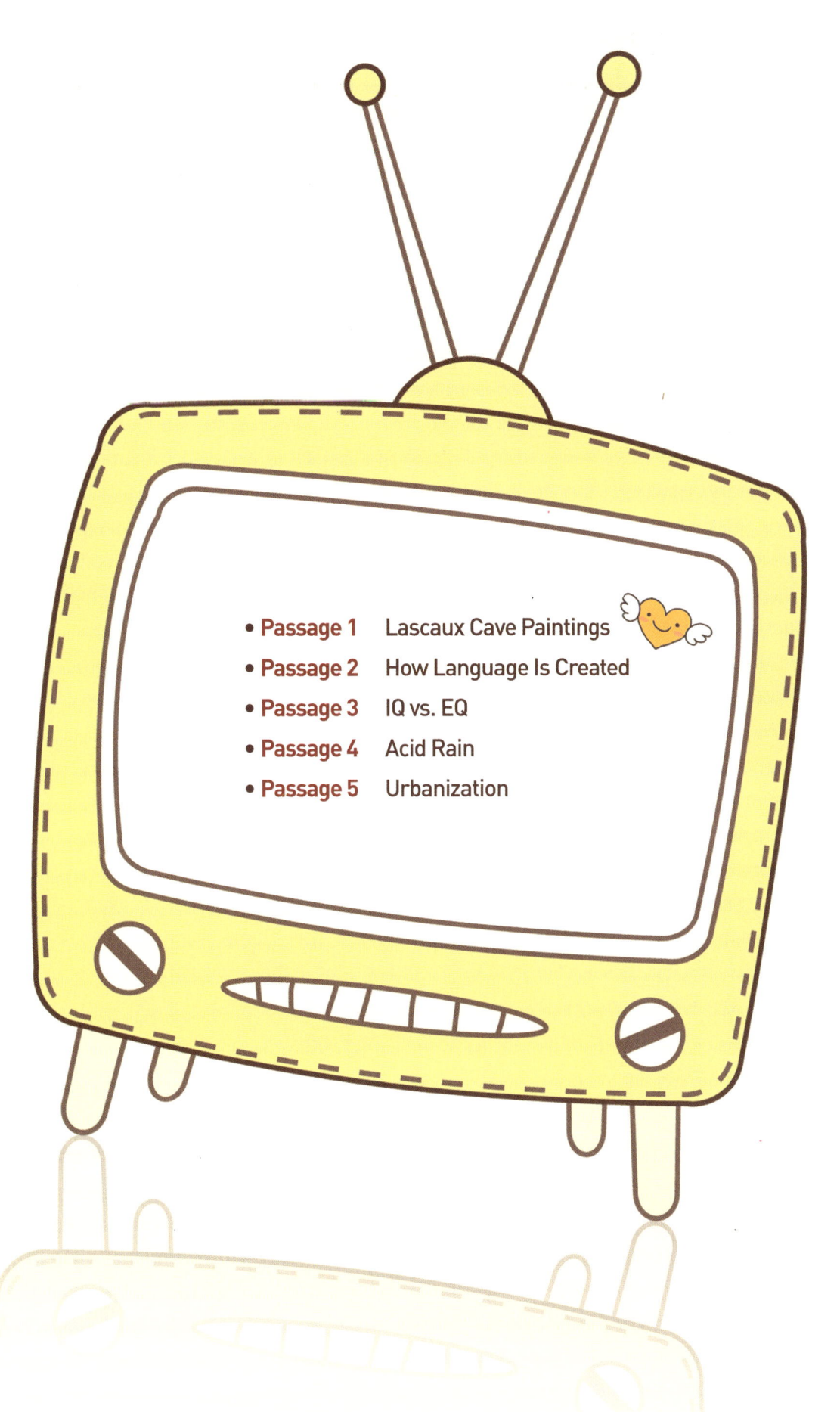

Passage 1

Lascaux Cave Paintings

In 1940, four French teenagers were exploring caves in southwestern France. Unexpectedly, they discovered ancient paintings in a cave. The cave is now called Lascaux. The walls of the cave are covered with hundreds of prehistoric paintings. Most of the images are realistic drawings of animals. Scientists hypothesize that the paintings are 16,000 years old.

Since the discovery of the paintings, thousands of people have visited the cave. [■A] Some people are fascinated by the art. The famous black bull painting is 17 feet long. [■B] It is the longest cave painting in the world. [■C] In addition, it demonstrates that the artist knew how to create the feeling of motion in the painting. [■D] This skill of creating perspective in art wasn't seen again until the 15th century. Other people, however, visit the cave because they are trying to understand the history of the people.

Many historians want to understand the life of people who lived 16,000 years ago. Among the 2,000 images, 900 of them have been identified as animals. Yet there are no images of reindeer despite them being a primary food source for prehistoric people. Bulls are the most dominant images present, and only one human image has been found. Historians wonder if animals had ritual meaning. Besides animals, there are also images of dots. Some historians think they represent stars seen from the Earth. Others believe they indicate a spiritual ritual. While many images are slowly disappearing, scientists, historians, and artists have learned a lot about our evolution from them.

hypothesize: to suppose, to provide a possible explanation on something
indicate: to show, to represent

1. Look at the four squares [■] that indicate where the following sentence could be added to the passage.

   People have different objectives in making visits to the cave.

   Where would the sentence best fit?

2. The word demonstrates in the passage is closest in meaning to

   Ⓐ expects
   Ⓑ says
   Ⓒ discovers
   Ⓓ shows

3. Why does the author say This skill of creating perspective in art wasn't seen again until the 15th century in paragraph 2?

   Ⓐ To show that the skills used in the cave paintings are fairly modern
   Ⓑ To emphasize the importance of making perspective in art
   Ⓒ To introduce the skills of painters in the 15th century in the following sentence
   Ⓓ To explain that the skills used in the cave paintings are unique

4. According to paragraphs 2 and 3, it can be inferred that

   Ⓐ the cave became popular because it had the longest cave painting in the world
   Ⓑ the paintings in the cave give clues about prehistoric people
   Ⓒ artists often recorded their history
   Ⓓ most of the paintings in the cave must be large

5. Which of the following best expresses the essential information in the highlighted sentence in the passage? Incorrect answer choices change the meaning in important ways or leave out essential information.

   Yet there are no images of reindeer despite them being a primary food source for prehistoric people.

   Ⓐ Reindeer were the food source for prehistoric people thus there are no paintings of them.
   Ⓑ Although there is no evidence, it is believed that prehistoric people ate reindeer.
   Ⓒ Although reindeer were an important food source for prehistoric people, there are no reindeer paintings.
   Ⓓ Prehistoric people didn't draw reindeer because they were an important food source.

6 The word dominant in the passage is closest in meaning to

Ⓐ powerful
Ⓑ interesting
Ⓒ common
Ⓓ popular

7 According to paragraphs 2 and 3, all of the following can be found in the Lascaux cave paintings EXCEPT

Ⓐ a human
Ⓑ stars
Ⓒ bulls
Ⓓ dots

8 The word them in the passage refers to

Ⓐ animals
Ⓑ images
Ⓒ effects
Ⓓ visitors

9 Directions: An introductory sentence for a brief summary of the passage is provided below. Complete the summary by selecting the THREE answer choices that express important ideas in the passage. Some sentences do not belong in the summary because they express ideas that are not presented in the passage or are minor ideas in the passage.

The Lascaux cave has a lot of prehistoric paintings that are 16,000 years old.

-
-
-

Answer Choices

Ⓐ The cave was unexpectedly discovered by four French teenagers in 1940.
Ⓑ The paintings of animals had ritual meaning in prehistoric times.
Ⓒ The cave is well-known for having the image of prehistoric people.
Ⓓ Thousands of people have visited the cave to study its art and history.
Ⓔ The paintings have enabled people to understand the life of prehistoric people.
Ⓕ Scientists think the paintings are 16,000 years old.

How Language Is Created

Language is a living and evolving thing. Daily, language is being created and modified to fit the needs of the humans. There are many ways new words are added to a language. Three common methods of word formation are through blending, back formation, and acronym formation.

[■A] Blending is the process of combining two already existing words. Blending occurs when a new activity or element needs to be named. [■B] An example is the word *smog*. This word, which means hazy, visible pollution in the air, is a combination of the words *smoke* and *fog*. In other cases, blending is used to describe what something is. [■C] Words like *mailbox* and *bedroom* are good examples of this type of blending. [■D]

Back formation also uses existing words to create other forms of speech. A new word is formed from a longer word by removing part of it. Thus, the new word is usually shorter than the original word. Back formation has given English the verbs *edit* from *editor*: *edit* looks like the source of *editor*, but it is the other way round. The verb *donate* is also made from the noun *donation*.

Acronyms are another way that new words are formed. The process of creating acronyms is not about creating a new concept. It simply provides shorter word references for longer groups of words. These words are often created by combining the first letter of each word from a phrase. For example, *AIDS* is the shortened form of autoimmune deficiency syndrome. In this way, people can speak more quickly and easily. Acronyms are also used for names of organizations that are too long to pronounce or write. Groups like *NATO* and *UNICEF* have been coined with acronyms because of their long names.

1 According to paragraph 1, language is alive in that

   Ⓐ it can be created and modified
   Ⓑ there are many ways to create a new language
   Ⓒ humans use it every day
   Ⓓ it is unchanging

2 The word combining in the passage is closest in meaning to

   Ⓐ joining
   Ⓑ separating
   Ⓒ using
   Ⓓ collecting

3 Look at the four squares [■] that indicate where the following sentence could be added to the passage.

   Blending, however, is not the only type of word formation that uses already existing words.

   Where would the sentence best fit?

4 Why does the author say *edit* looks like the source of *editor*, but it is the other way round in paragraph 3?

   Ⓐ To give an example of back formation
   Ⓑ To point out the fact that readers might not know
   Ⓒ To emphasize the relations between the two words, *edit* and *editor*
   Ⓓ To explain how the word *edit* is formed

5 According to paragraph 3, back formation

   Ⓐ uses two existing words
   Ⓑ occurs when people need to name a new thing
   Ⓒ creates other forms of speech
   Ⓓ produces *editor* from *edit*

6 The word coined in the passage is closest in meaning to

  Ⓐ processed
  Ⓑ arranged
  Ⓒ made
  Ⓓ changed

7 The word their in the passage refers to

  Ⓐ people
  Ⓑ names
  Ⓒ groups
  Ⓓ acronyms

8 **Directions**: Complete the table below about the word formation processes discussed in the passage. Match the statements to the appropriate category with which they are associated. TWO of the answer choices will NOT be used.

Answer Choices

Ⓐ Organization names are good examples of this process.

Ⓑ It is a process for making a new idea.

Ⓒ It uses the first letter of each word from a phrase.

Ⓓ It makes shorter expressions longer.

Ⓔ The word *smog* is an example of this process.

Ⓕ It means combining two existing words.

Ⓖ People can pronounce the word created by this process easily and quickly.

Acronym

- _____
- _____
- _____

Blending

- _____
- _____

Passage 3

IQ vs. EQ

In the past, measuring a person's intelligence was based on a single standard: IQ (Intelligence Quotient). [■A] Tests that measure IQ usually examine a person's memory. [■B] Yet researchers found that many people with high IQs were still not successful in life. [■C] For example, some CEOs did not have IQs as high as some of their employees. [■D] In addition, those with high IQs were not necessarily happier than those with low IQs. Due to these puzzling facts, researchers began searching for another type of intelligence that humans possess.

The concept of the EQ (Emotional Quotient) was introduced in the early 1990s. EQ is a type of social and emotional intelligence. Having a high EQ allows people to understand both others and themselves better. More surprising was the discovery that those with high EQs were usually more satisfied and successful in life. EQ, more than IQ, seems to be connected to success. It is related to self-motivation and the successful pursuit of goals. While natural ability (IQ) can help one achieve goals, without motivation they will never succeed. But can a person change his IQ or EQ?

Unfortunately, IQ is stable. A person is born with a certain capacity for learning and often has difficulty changing that ability. However, EQ is intelligence that can be developed throughout life. One develops EQ through activities like learning to make friends. EQ also affects IQ. While a person may be naturally smart, if they feel depressed, they will often have difficulty completing tasks. In this way, it is clear that having a high EQ is more connected with a person's happiness and success in life than having a high IQ.

1. Look at the four squares [■] that indicate where the following sentence could be added to the passage.

   How quickly a person learns and how they apply what they learn are also tested.

   Where would the sentence best fit?

2. The word possess in the passage is closest in meaning to
   - Ⓐ host
   - Ⓑ show
   - Ⓒ use
   - Ⓓ have

3. The word connected in the passage is closest in meaning to
   - Ⓐ linked
   - Ⓑ fixed
   - Ⓒ moved
   - Ⓓ matched

4. The word achieve in the passage is closest in meaning to
   - Ⓐ recognize
   - Ⓑ choose
   - Ⓒ obtain
   - Ⓓ review

5. Why does the author say But can a person change his IQ or EQ? in paragraph 2?
   - Ⓐ To introduce the topic of the following paragraph
   - Ⓑ To prove that a person can change their IQ or EQ
   - Ⓒ To emphasize that both IQ and EQ cannot be changed
   - Ⓓ To make readers think about this question

6 According to the passage, those with high EQs

    Ⓐ tend to have high IQs
    Ⓑ are naturally smart
    Ⓒ tend to make friends easily
    Ⓓ are not successful in life

7 Which of the following best expresses the essential information in the highlighted sentence in the passage? Incorrect answer choices change the meaning in important ways or leave out essential information.

> In this way, it is clear that having a high EQ is more connected with a person's happiness and success in life than having a high IQ.

    Ⓐ It is clear that people can feel happiness and achieve success in life by having a high IQ.
    Ⓑ There's no question that EQ has more to do with one's happiness and success in life than one's IQ.
    Ⓒ People with a high IQ can be more successful and happier in life than those with a high EQ.
    Ⓓ It is true that a high EQ brings success and happiness in one's life.

8 **Directions**: Complete the table below about EQ and IQ discussed in the passage. Match the appropriate statements to the types with which they are associated. TWO of the answer choices will NOT be used.

Answer Choices

    Ⓐ It is hard to change.
    Ⓑ It can be developed over time.
    Ⓒ Low scores in this area guarantee a successful life.
    Ⓓ It indicates social and emotional intelligence.
    Ⓔ The concept was introduced in the 1990s.
    Ⓕ It cannot be measured.
    Ⓖ It usually measures a person's memory.

EQ
-
-
-

IQ
-
-

Passage 4

Acid Rain

Acid rain is any form of rain that contains acids. The acids in acid rain come from the many chemical particles that exist in the atmosphere. These exist largely because of human pollution. Acid rain is becoming an increasing problem around the world. It has been causing health problems for people, the destruction of forests and plant life, and deadly changes in water ecosystems.

Acid rain has made humans encounter an increasing number of health problems. Since the beginning of the acid rain problem, more and more chemical particles have been present in the air. People breathe in these particles and many of them remain in the lungs. [■A] Often, these particles can be the main cause of lung cancer. [■B] They can also cause heart problems. [■C] A recent study reported that between 22,000 and 52,000 deaths occur per year in the United States due to acid rain. [■D]

The environment has been suffering from the effects of acid rain as well. Plants and trees have been experiencing more damage because of acid rain. For example, calcium has been slowly removed from trees. Nutrient removal like this can cause trees to be more easily damaged by cold weather. Trees are dying earlier than expected because of chemicals introduced by acid rain. The damage to food crops is also harmful to humans.

Water life has also been greatly changed by the introduction of acid rain. Large amounts of acid rain have lowered the pH of lakes and streams. At pH levels of 5, fish eggs often won't hatch. Lower pH levels can kill adult fish. Acid rain has also eliminated many insect populations. Fish that rely on these insects for food have also died. Humans depend on fish as a food source. If humans don't take measures to decrease the chemicals creating acid rain, they may destroy their environment along with their own health.

encounter: to experience, to undergo
hatch: to come out of an egg

1 According to paragraph 1, all of the following are mentioned as a result of acid rain EXCEPT

  Ⓐ human health problems
  Ⓑ harmful effects on forests and plants
  Ⓒ the destruction of buildings
  Ⓓ negative changes in water life

2 The word them in the passage refers to

  Ⓐ humans
  Ⓑ problems
  Ⓒ particles
  Ⓓ lungs

3 Look at the four squares [■] that indicate where the following sentence could be added to the passage.

  In addition, these particles can pass from the lungs to other parts of the body.

  Where would the sentence best fit?

4 According to paragraph 3, if plants lack calcium

  Ⓐ they can die
  Ⓑ they lose their ability to survive in cold weather
  Ⓒ they can become harmful to humans
  Ⓓ they can damage other plants around them

5 Which of the following best expresses the essential information in the highlighted sentence in the passage? Incorrect answer choices change the meaning in important ways or leave out essential information.

> Water life has also been greatly changed by the introduction of acid rain.

Ⓐ Acid rain has also changed the life of underwater organisms a lot.
Ⓑ Water animals have been affected by a great deal of rain.
Ⓒ Acid rain has caused a lot of problems in the ecosystem.
Ⓓ Acid rain has resulted in some changes to water animals.

6 The word eliminated in the passage is closest in meaning to

Ⓐ increased
Ⓑ scattered
Ⓒ killed
Ⓓ affected

7 Why does the author mention insect populations in paragraph 4?

Ⓐ To show how acid rain can affect the food chain
Ⓑ To explain that some fish rely on insects for food
Ⓒ To emphasize the amount of chemicals that humans have produced
Ⓓ To show the effects of acid rain on land

8 The word decrease in the passage is closest in meaning to

Ⓐ hold
Ⓑ weaken
Ⓒ use
Ⓓ lower

9 Directions: An introductory sentence for a brief summary of the passage is provided below. Complete the summary by selecting the THREE answer choices that express important ideas in the passage. Some sentences do not belong in the summary because they express ideas that are not presented in the passage or are minor ideas in the passage.

Acid rain has caused problems in humans' health, forests, and water ecosystems.

-
-
-

Answer Choices

Ⓐ Acid rain will eventually make people die.
Ⓑ Humans have encountered many health problems due to acid rain.
Ⓒ The role of calcium is very important in the growth of plants.
Ⓓ Acid rain has damaged plants and trees.
Ⓔ The introduction of acid rain has changed the lives of organisms in water.
Ⓕ The pH level of water is important to the survival of water animals.

Passage 5

Urbanization

Throughout most of history, humans have lived a rural lifestyle. In the last 100 years, however, the world's population has become increasingly urbanized. Urbanization is the process of many people moving to the same areas of a country, creating cities. In 1950, the population of only 83 cities exceeded one million. By 2007, this had risen to 468 cities.

There are two primary factors for recent urbanization. One is population increase and the other is an increase in people moving to urban areas. [■A] As the availability of food and medicine increases, the growth rate of the population increases. [■B] Due to an increase in population, areas that were once rural have become urban. [■C] In the past, people were needed mostly for agriculture. [■D] However, as society advances, more people are moving to cities to be educated and get jobs. These jobs offer better salaries, and these higher salaries offer a more comfortable lifestyle.

Increased urbanization is usually seen as advancement. However, urbanization creates several problems. Increases in traffic, increased pollution, and the destruction of the environment are three major problems of urbanization. With cities growing so rapidly, governments are having difficulty providing services for all of the people who live in cities. Additionally, urbanization has been followed by an increase in poverty as well.

City governments are trying to solve the negative effects of urbanization. Public transportation has become increasingly popular in cities. Also, boundaries have been created around natural areas to protect the environment in many cities. Finally, several countries have created programs for the homeless. When cities take care of people's basic needs, many of the poor are able to find jobs. The numbers of big cities are still on the rise. Yet slowly, cities are learning how to deal with the problems of ever-growing cities.

exceed: to be larger or greater than something

1 According to paragraph 1, one of the main factors for recent urbanization
   Ⓐ is the population increase in rural areas
   Ⓑ is the change from a rural lifestyle to an urban lifestyle
   Ⓒ is the movement of people to urban areas
   Ⓓ is creating cities in rural areas

2 Look at the four squares [■] that indicate where the following sentence could be added to the passage.

   This means more people are healthy enough to have children, and less people are dying.

   Where would the sentence best fit?

3 The word advances in the passage is closest in meaning to
   Ⓐ develops
   Ⓑ experiences
   Ⓒ appears
   Ⓓ begins

4 The word offer in the passage is closest in meaning to
   Ⓐ include
   Ⓑ provide
   Ⓒ require
   Ⓓ make

5 According to paragraph 3, which of the following is NOT mentioned as a problem of urbanization?

Ⓐ poverty
Ⓑ the destruction of the environment
Ⓒ pollution
Ⓓ a lack of jobs

6 According to paragraph 4, which of the following is NOT mentioned as a way city governments have been trying to solve the negative effects of urbanization?

Ⓐ Creating homeless programs
Ⓑ Protecting natural areas
Ⓒ Encouraging people to use public transportation
Ⓓ Creating many jobs for the poor

7 Which of the following best expresses the essential information in the highlighted sentence in the passage? Incorrect answer choices change the meaning in important ways or leave out essential information.

> Yet slowly, cities are learning how to deal with the problems of ever-growing cities.

Ⓐ However, cities are learning the way to solve the problems of a developing society.
Ⓑ On the other hand, many countries find ways to solve the problems of urbanization.
Ⓒ However, cities will solve the problems slowly.
Ⓓ Although it might be slow, cities are learning how to handle the urbanization problems.

8 Directions: An introductory sentence for a brief summary of the passage is provided below. Complete the summary by selecting the THREE answer choices that express important ideas in the passage. Some sentences do not belong in the summary because they express ideas that are not presented in the passage or are minor ideas in the passage.

Urbanization is the process through which the world's population is becoming urbanized.

-
-
-

Answer Choices

Ⓐ Population growth and an increase in people moving to urban areas are the two main causes of urbanization.
Ⓑ An increase in population has created more rural areas in the world.
Ⓒ Urbanization can be seen as development, but it also causes problems.
Ⓓ The use of public transportation will solve the problems of urbanization.
Ⓔ The growth of urban populations cannot be stopped.
Ⓕ City governments are trying to solve the problems of urbanization.

Wit&Wisdom iBT TOEFL Series

Beginning (40~60) · Intermediate (60~90)

The iBT TOEFL Beginner Series

 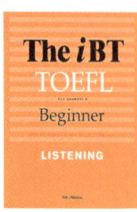  

★ **The iBT TOEFL Beginner**
Reading / Listening / Speaking / Writing

Perium VOCA Series

★★ **Perium VOCA for TOEFL**
Reading / Speaking / Writing

The iBT TOEFL Series

★★ **The iBT TOEFL**
Reading / Listening / Speaking / Writing

The iBT Grammar Series

★★ **The iBT Grammar**
for Beginners / for All Learners / Practice Test

Wit&Wisdom iBT TOEFL Series

Advanced (90~110)

The iBT TOEFL Solution Series

★★★
The iBT TOEFL Solution
Reading / Listening / Speaking / Writing

The iBT TOEFL Master Series

★★★★
The iBT TOEFL Master
Reading / Listening / Speaking / Writing

The iBT TOEFL Actual Test Series

★★★
The iBT TOEFL Actual Test
Vol. 1 / Vol. 2 / Vol. 3